THE EDGE OF LEADERSHIP

THE EDGE OF LEADERSHIP

FIGHT FOR CHILDREN
NO MATTER THE COST

by

DR. BERNARD GASSAWAY

Contents

Part III: Reflections From the Edge

Part IV: Published Works

DEDICATION

TO Baba Stanley Kinard—my friend, colleague, confidant, and mentor.

I first met Baba Stan through the legendary Frank Mickens, who always spoke of him with deep admiration and respect. It was Baba Stan who recommended Mickens to be a Revson Fellow at Columbia University—a gesture that would later ripple into my own life when Mickens, in turn, recommended me for the same honor. That connection marked the beginning of a transformative relationship.

When I became principal of Boys and Girls High School, I knew I needed someone by my side who truly understood both the soul of the community and the moral clarity required to lead it. I hired Baba Stan, and he quickly became my most trusted confidant and thought partner. Every morning, before the day's chaos set in, we met to discuss strategy, purpose, and the weight of the work ahead. He grounded me. He guided me. He challenged me.

More than anyone else, Baba Stan introduced me to the deep, often unseen, grassroots networks that pulse through Bedford-Stuyvesant. His insights were never just academic—they were lived, earned, and deeply rooted in love for the people.

I dedicate this book to his enduring legacy of truth, leadership, and community.

I Understand the Source of my Flame

My Mother's Love

NOTE TO READERS

Lead with love. There is no greater force!

Acknowledgments

I thank God for using me as a vessel to deliver hope and opportunities for children, families, and communities.

I thank and adore my beautiful and brilliant, caring and courageous daughter, Atiya Lilly-Gassaway.

I thank my wife, Angela Gassaway, for breathing life into me. She entered my life at a critical time—when I was looking for a tree to rest and read.

I also thank Angela for being an inspiration to write this book. She encouraged me to share parts of my journey so future leaders can better understand how to lead from the edge.

Don't lose the lesson in the struggle.

—Bernard Gassaway

PREFACE

I believe in the power of storytelling. I have been listening to and telling stories since I was a child. You learn early on how to distinguish between truth and fact.

When I reflect on my childhood, particularly my years in New York City public schools, I do not have many positive experiences. Starting from middle school, I could name one teacher with whom I connected, none in elementary. I had several teachers with whom I connected in high school. The most memorable was my physical education teacher, Mr. Horace Jones.

I attended a school for trouble boys—Sterling High School. Many of us were court-involved and, rightly or wrongly, classified as students in need of special education services. The unofficial title for our school was a 600 school. These schools eventually gave birth to what is currently known as District 75 schools.

With the support of dedicated teachers at Sterling High School, my mother, my supportive sister, Denise, and brother-in-law, Ralph Gaston, I managed to get accepted to LeMoyne College in Syracuse, NY.

Interestingly, after graduating from college and graduate school, I decided to become a teacher shortly after my mother's death in 1986. My mother would be shocked to know that I became a teacher—largely motivated by her unwavering love for me and my siblings.

It is my childhood experiences, and later adult experiences, in the New York City public school system that inspired me to share these stories, letters, speeches and reflections in this book. My purpose is to inspire and encourage current educators to connect with the Bernards in their schools and communities and be a positive and motivating force in their lives. One day, they may then become teachers, assistant principals, principals, superintendents, community advocates, or entrepreneurs.

INTRODUCTION

I have often heard the advice: *"Bernard, you have to pick your battles."* While I agree with this wisdom, I have also learned that when you lead from the edge, sometimes the battle picks you. The personal stories and reflections I share in this book highlight some of the most profound and impactful battles that chose me. Perhaps I had the option to walk away, but at the root of nearly every battle was one central truth: doing what was right for children.

Many have spoken of the "children first" mantra, but I believed it, lived it, and practiced it. When it came to deciding whether to fight for children, I felt I had no choice. My very existence demanded that I engage in the struggle—no matter the cost.

Never once, when standing up for children, did I pause to ask myself, *"What if I lose my job?"* That thought never entered my calculations. This does not mean I was reckless. It means I believed deeply that no leader should ever place personal financial security above the security and well-being of children. For those who lead from the edge, facing job loss is not an abstract fear—it is a lived reality. The price of fighting for children can be painfully high.

When speaking with aspiring school and district leaders, I often pose a simple but difficult question: *"What is your price?"* After a pause, I follow with a sharper one: *"How much would it cost you to look the other way while children are being harmed under your watch?"*

Behind every story in this book lie lessons, questions, and messages. I chose to share these experiences not only to reflect on my own journey, but to offer readers an opportunity for self-examination: *What might I have done differently, if anything? How can I apply these insights to my own practice as a leader? How can I find the courage to lead from the edge—to fight for students to have the best possible educational experience?*

Leading from the edge does not sugarcoat reality. It forces leaders—especially in urban schools—to confront the harsh truths that many would rather ignore. The ultimate question is this: When children are being miseducated, which is no different than being harmed, will you look the other way? Or will you find the courage to step to the edge and fight?

PART I

ADVOCACY AND PUBLIC VOICE

Fundamental to any system is the design dictates the results.

—Bernard Gassaway

BLOOMBERG,
IT IS NOT TOO LATE

IN my second year as principal of Boys and Girls High School, Mayor Bloomberg hired Cathleen "Cathie" Black to replace Joel Klein as New York City's Public Schools Chancellor. By all accounts, Cathie Black was not qualified to serve as chancellor, not to mention she did not hold any of the required certifications to serve in this role. Surely this was an ill-advised decision by Bloomberg. I was curious if he would ever admit it. Her tenure as chancellor only lasted 95 days. Bloomberg's ability and authority to hire Black was a clear display of the power of mayoral control. In full disclosure, I was an advocate for mayoral control of public schools at this time. I was so baffled by Bloomberg's decision to hire Black; so, I wrote him a letter. This was bold of me because if he read it, he or his chancellor could have found a reason to remove me—I did not care. I share this letter in hopes that you may find strength in truth and advocacy—even if it may cost you your job or freedom in more extreme cases.

Originally Published 2011

Dear Mr. Bloomberg,

    My name is Bernard Gassaway, proud father of

16-year-old Atiya Lilly-Gassaway. I am a doctoral candidate at Teachers College, and my dissertation topic is "Principal as Community Leader." I believe that principals must serve as de facto community leaders if they are to faithfully serve their children. When I agreed to serve as principal of Boys and Girls High School, I was clear about the challenges. I knew that I would likely face many battles with children, teachers, parents, and community stakeholders. My job, like yours, is complicated. I can relate to you when you strongly believe in a position, regardless of the opposition.

The purpose of my letter is to highlight some things you may want to consider as your tenure as mayor comes to a close, particularly with respect to the New York City Department of Education and your legacy as the education mayor. I beg your indulgence as I share some of my thoughts about our system of education and the role you may be able to play in creating sustainable change.

Mr. Bloomberg, it is not too late. You can build political capital and respect by saying, "I was wrong to select Cathie Black as chancellor without community input." Many see that selection as more of an exercise of political muscle than political maturity. No one, at this point in your mayoralty, should question your strength. You have crushed all of your critics, rendering most impotent. They may call you arrogant and stubborn. So what! You still have the final word. Some people may refer to you as being "gangster." In some circles, this is an expression of respect. As a sign of self-respect, I recommend, again, that you demonstrate contrition and admit your error in the way you handled the chancellor selection.

Mr. Bloomberg, I agree with your espoused position that every child should have a highly effective teacher. To this end, I will fight with you. I may agree with other policies that you have implemented. However, I strongly disagree with your tinkering with your democracy. When you fire anyone who votes against your position (as you did with your battle for the elimination of social promotion), you create fear and paralysis. Your approach does not allow for evidence or reason to prevail. You have closed some schools in the face of convincing opposition. As I watched the school closing hearings, I often wondered why members of the public participated. Didn't they know that you had decided to close the schools months before the actual hearing? Didn't they know the actual hearings were merely perfunctory? All of the screaming and gesticulations were wasted, though valiant acts. At the end of the day, I feel badly for the children. The closing of their schools, without true due process, may have tainted any understanding of democracy that they learned in school.

Mr. Bloomberg, it is not too late for you to make a few changes in your policies and practices to become the true education mayor. Ultimately, you want to build a sustainable school system. Some of the good that you have done may dissipate as soon as you leave office. This is what happens to many schools once "savior principals" leave. All that they have worked to establish is undone by their successors. Why? They did not understand the principles of sustainable leadership. If you find the time, read "Seven Principles of Sustainable Leadership" by Andy Hargreaves and Dean Fink.

Mr. Bloomberg, I am not interested in joining the chorus of folks who scream and shout in opposition to your policies and practices, specifically your pledge to open an unprecedented number of charter schools or your failure to faithfully engage the public in meaningful policy discussions. Although some agree with some of your actions vis-à-vis education, many, including me, do not agree with your Machiavellian approach: The end does not always justify the means. I would recommend that you earnestly engage some of our preeminent scholars on school reform in ongoing analysis of our school system. The time is right for such analysis. I would also recommend that you engage community stakeholders in unprecedented ways. Invite the communities to establish independent think tanks to discuss and recommend policies and practices. Your current leadership approach absolves the community of its inherent obligation to educate its children. No school is an island. No community is an island. All are inextricably connected in one way or another. Since people are afraid of you, they sit back and silently criticize your policies and practices while failing to take meaningful actions of their own.

Mr. Bloomberg, it is not too late to establish a legacy as the education mayor if you transform your approach and let the democratic process prevail. Unfortunately, your current legacy may reveal that you used your political might to muffle democracy by dismissing the very pillars that support our society. You should not lead as if your followers are peons or minions. It is true that many folks are afraid of you. They fear your wrath and fury. They witness what you do to those who disagree with you. History may reveal that you were not unlike dictators who ruled with fear and an iron fist. Mr. Bloomberg, embrace democracy over dictatorship. It is not too late to change your ways.

Mr. Bloomberg, when we look at great leaders of the past, all have undergone some form of personal transformation. Demonstrate a willingness to accept sound advice. Use the remainder of your time in office to allow independent researchers to study the impact of your policies and practices. On the one hand, place a moratorium on school closings, particularly on schools that have rich traditions in their communities. On the other, continue to pursue policies that would allow principals to immediately remove ineffective staff from schools, with swift and deliberate due process.

You may silence your critics by inviting them to propose better solutions than the ones that you currently dictate. By doing so, you may help to establish sustainable change that may last far beyond your tenure as mayor.

Let your legacy be that you began the real revolution in education. You fought for the right of every child in New York City to have a highly effective teacher in his or her classroom. It is not too late.

[I do not know if he read the letter. I do know that he did not respond privately or publicly.]

It was a stark reminder that leadership in public education is often a balancing act between data-driven decision-making and political appeasement.

—Bernard Gassaway

LEADERSHIP LESSONS FROM THE GED SITE CLOSURES

IN September of 2004, while serving as Superintendent of District 79 in the New York City Public Schools, I found myself confronting one of the most politically and emotionally charged challenges of my career. District 79 served as the educational home for students in alternative programs, including incarcerated youth, pregnant and parenting teens, and students pursuing General Educational Development (GED) diplomas. My leadership was predicated on transparency, accountability, and above all, student outcomes. When I began to assess the state of GED programs across the city, I quickly realized that a system meant to serve some of our most vulnerable students had become stagnant, inefficient, and, in many cases, obsolete.

Through direct consultation with school officials and firsthand observation, I discovered that many of the GED sites across the city were operating far below capacity. This was not merely an administrative inefficiency; it was a systemic issue that had implications for funding, staffing, and, most importantly, student success. I vividly recall visiting an evening site on Hillside Avenue in Jamaica, Queens. The school building was dimly lit, and not a single student was in attendance. I found the teacher in her classroom, calmly working on lesson plans for her day job in a traditional high school. Her GED teaching assignment was a per-session role, and it was clear that no students were expected to attend that evening. I asked her why she wasn't reaching out to students, and she replied with disarming candor: she was simply doing what she had always done.

That encounter crystallized for me the nature of the problem. The system had calcified. Teachers were being paid to supervise empty rooms, while students who genuinely needed educational opportunities were nowhere to be found. These GED programs were originally designed to offer flexible, alternative pathways for students who had disengaged from traditional schools. But the reality was that many of the sites had become ceremonial placeholders, maintained more out of habit than necessity.

Armed with this insight, I brought my concerns to Chancellor Joel Klein and other senior Department of Education (DOE) officials. We analyzed attendance data and determined that daily attendance at many evening GED sites hovered below 40 percent. In some cases, entire buildings were opened and staffed for just one or two students. We knew we could no longer justify the fiscal and human resource expenditures, particularly when those resources could be redirected to more impactful programming.

Together, we developed a plan to consolidate and close several underperforming GED sites. It was not a decision taken lightly. We anticipated resistance and planned for community engagement. However, the press would soon derail our careful planning. *The New York Times* ran a story titled "Help Sites for Dropouts Are Closed," which portrayed the closures as an abrupt, callous move that abandoned at-risk youth. The reporting, in my opinion, was biased and not always accurate. The nuances of low attendance, fiscal inefficiency, and plans for alternative support structures were omitted or misrepresented.

Shortly after the article was published, I was interviewed by ABC's local television news. I reiterated the rationale for the closures, highlighting our commitment to reallocating resources to programs that demonstrated real student engagement. Still, the backlash was swift and vocal. Community advocates, some educators, and especially the press, seized upon the closures as symbolic of systemic neglect.

To my surprise and dismay, some of the very DOE officials who had collaborated on the decision began to distance themselves from the plan. Whether due to political pressure or fear of public reprisal, they left me holding the proverbial bag. I had taken ownership of the plan because it was grounded in data and designed with students in mind. Yet, in the court of public opinion, I was cast as the villain.

I will never forget the day I walked into a staff meeting with the entire Auxiliary Services High Schools staff. It looked to be at least one hundred teachers and support staff. As I was introduced, a loud and unified "Boo" rang out across the auditorium. It was a stunning moment, but I did not flinch. Leadership requires the ability to withstand public criticism when it is rooted in a commitment to doing what is right, not what is popular.

I calmly explained the rationale for the GED site closures. I spoke about the low attendance rates, the wasted resources, and the opportunity to reinvest in programs with greater reach and impact. Slowly, the energy in the room began to shift. Some educators nodded in agreement; they knew the truth. They had witnessed firsthand the dysfunction and underutilization that plagued many of the evening sites. In private conversations after the meeting, a few even thanked me for saying what they had long known but were afraid to admit.

However, the political fallout was not over. Then-City Council Education Chair Eva Moskowitz publicly criticized the DOE for the way the closures were handled. Her concerns were not unfounded. In hindsight, I recognize that our communication strategy was flawed. We had failed to build a strong narrative before the closures took place. We underestimated the emotional and symbolic importance of these sites to certain communities and failed to engage stakeholders early enough in the process.

In response to political and community pressure, DOE officials directed me to reinstate some of the closed GED sites. These decisions were not based on new data or a reversal of rationale; they were driven purely by political expediency. While I complied with the directive, I did so with a sense of disillusionment. It was a stark reminder that leadership in public education is often a balancing act between data-driven decision-making and political appeasement.

Reflecting on this experience, I have come to appreciate the depth of the leadership lessons it offered. First, transparency and communication are essential, not just in the execution of change but in the planning phase. Stakeholders must feel that they are part of the conversation, even if they disagree with the outcome. Second, leaders must be prepared to stand alone. When the storm comes, and it will come, you must have the integrity to weather it. Finally, change is rarely welcomed with open arms. Even when change is clearly beneficial, people cling to the familiar. That resistance must be anticipated, respected, and addressed with empathy.

The decision to close GED evening sites in New York City in 2004 was not a failure of leadership; it was, in many ways, a test of it. I stood by the data, the rationale, and the students who deserved better. But I also learned that leadership cannot exist in a vacuum. It requires collaboration, communication, and sometimes, the humility to admit that even the right decisions can be poorly received if not properly conveyed.

In the end, this experience did not break me. It sharpened me. It made me more deliberate in how I engage communities, more strategic in how I manage stakeholder relationships, and more courageous in my convictions. It reinforced for me that leadership is not about avoiding mistakes; it's about learning from them, growing through them, and emerging stronger on the other side.

As educators and leaders, we are often asked to navigate the complex intersection of policy, practice, and politics. We must make decisions that serve students, even when those decisions are unpopular. And we must do so with a deep sense of purpose, clarity, and resolve. That is the essence of true leadership.

Sometimes, the dues we pay to maintain integrity are pretty high, but the ultimate cost of moral compromise is much higher.

—Michael Josephson

COST OF INTEGRITY: EXPOSING THE QUIET SCANDAL

TWICE a year, we distributed transcripts to students so they could begin to take accountability for their academic progress. In high school, course credits are the students' currency—alongside passing state-mandated completion exams known as the Regents.

On one occasion, after distributing the transcripts, I noticed a student peering intensely at her grades. With surprise and consternation, she exclaimed, "I passed!" Curious, I asked her what happened. She had passed two of the most difficult Regents exams—Global Studies and U.S. History—with scores of 85 and 90, respectively. Until this point, she had failed every attempt.

My curiosity turned into concern. Upon reviewing other transcripts for students classified as students with disabilities, I found that approximately 60 students with a history of repeated failure had also suddenly passed, with scores consistently above 80. This wasn't a fluke. It suggested something more deliberate.

My immediate suspicion wasn't the students—but the adults. I filed a formal complaint with the NYC

Department of Education's Office of Special Investigations (OSI).

Nearly a year passed without a word. Eventually, we were informed that the State Education Department had selected our school for a Regents exam audit. That in itself wasn't alarming—routine audits were common.

However, it quickly escalated. I learned that the state had notified OSI to investigate *me*, the principal, due to what they described as scoring irregularities. Soon after, an OSI investigator arrived at my school, stating plainly that he was there to investigate allegations of cheating.

Ironically, I had been the one to report the issue in the first place.

He confirmed that 57 of the 59 exam scores were reversed—from passing to failing—by the state audit. Someone had clearly inflated student performance. He acknowledged that I had previously filed the complaint and assured me that I had nothing to worry about. His investigation began with interviews in the Social Studies department. I suspected the assistant principal was the source of the issue.

Previously, the assistant principal had been removed from Boys and Girls High School. He was later hired by a principal in Queens—despite my direct warning. I had personally reached out to the new principal, but he refused to receive or even consider my evaluation.

At the time, grading Regents exams was done *in-house*, making it much easier to manipulate scores—a practice commonly referred to as "scrubbing."

A year later, when my school administered the Regents exams again under close scrutiny, our passing rates plummeted. Conversely, at the assistant principal's new school in Queens, the passing rates skyrocketed. The common denominator? The same assistant principal.

The state even assigned a staffer to monitor *me* throughout the day. I said to her, "You should be in Queens following the person who allegedly cheated when he was here."

My concerns were later validated. On April 13, 2013, *The New York Post* reported:

"When the city Department of Education rescored 25 'passing' global-history Regents exams at Mathematics, Science Research and Technology Magnet High School, all but one were found to have deserved a failing score."

That school was where the assistant principal had landed after leaving my school.

Shockingly, the school's report card rating remained unaffected by the cheating scandal.

That experience reinforced one painful truth: The New York City Department of Education didn't seem to care if principals cheated to boost performance metrics— as long as they didn't get caught.

The system rewarded results, even when they were fraudulent. Integrity, it seemed, was optional.

Education is the most powerful weapon which you can use to change the world.

—Nelson Mandela

Nelson Mandela: I Refused to Play

I remember sitting in my car, on December 5, 2013, about to drive from visiting my doctor in Freeport, NY. My phone rang, and I recognized the number immediately. It was Chancellor Dennis Walcott. [While I do not recall the telephone conversation verbatim, it went something like this]:

"Hello," he said. "I'm calling about what we plan to do following the death of Nelson Mandela."

I recall not feeling easy about talking about Nelson Mandela because he had just died early that day.

Then he continued.

"Mayor Bloomberg and I are holding a press conference tomorrow morning at Boys and Girls High School. We're going to announce the creation of a new high school in Mandela's honor. We want you there."

As he spoke, something in me hardened. I knew Mandela had visited Boys and Girls High School back in June 1990. I remembered the power of that moment—our students and community standing on the football field, eyes wide, hanging onto every word of a man who had just been released after 27 years in prison. That day was not just a moment in time—it was an imprint on our

23

collective soul. Mandela's presence had given our school and community a sense of global purpose.

But this? This phone call didn't feel like a tribute. It felt like politics.

After I hung up the phone, I sat in the silence of my car. The heater hummed, but the chill in my chest remained. I picked the phone back up and called Chancellor Walcott.

"I won't be attending the press conference," I said.

He paused. "May I ask why?"

"I won't be part of what I see as a political maneuver," I told him. "This is not the way to honor Mandela's legacy. It's opportunism." I was very firm in what I believe—that Mayor Bloomberg used Mandela's death for his own advantage. This was not about honoring our global hero.

That night, sleep didn't come easy. My mind ran in loops. Had I done the right thing? Would my decision come at a cost? But I knew one thing for certain: respect is not just about gestures—it's about process. And nothing about this felt respectful.

Prior to returning to Boys and Girls High School in 2009 as principal, I had served there as a teacher from 1988 to 1991. Before stepping into the principalship, I spoke with Principal Frank Mickens about his vision of creating small schools housed within Boys and Girls High School (BGHS). He had foreseen the school's declining student enrollment—something I believe was deliberately orchestrated by City Hall and the Department of Education. In my view, the strategy to "take over" BGHS was to gradually engineer conditions that would result in the school's ultimate failure.

I came back to BGHS with a mission. I firmly believed that my purpose there was to thwart those plans—to keep the school alive, and to keep it from being closed, which I ultimately accomplished. Because of its large size, the building had become a target, seen as a prime location for multiple co-located schools, including charter institutions. But while Principal Mickens was alive, no such overt plan could unfold without his endorsement. His standing in the community was simply too strong.

So, when critics and DOE officials propagated the idea that I opposed small schools in the building, they were wrong. What I opposed was the DOE implementing their plans in isolation—without community consultation, without honoring the legacy and labor that had gone into preserving this institution.

The narrative that I was against a school being named after Nelson Mandela was only partly true. I had no issue with honoring Mandela—in fact, I thought he deserved a much higher honor than the rushed, politically convenient naming of a school. What I took issue with was the timing and the intent. Mandela's death was used as a political strategy to advance an agenda that had been long in motion. His passing merely gave city officials a palatable path forward.

After the Nelson Mandela School for Social Justice was officially established, the challenges continued. The administration of the new school struggled to recruit a sufficient number of students to open in September 2014. In response, the DOE Chancellor placed a moratorium on Boys and Girls High School enrollment. Students whom we had painstakingly recruited were redirected to the Mandela school—without our consent.

I wrote an email to Chancellor Carmen Fariña, voicing my concerns and protest. That message remains a documented part of my resistance.

Community members began to speak out. Parents who had been deeply invested in Boys and Girls High School for years expressed outrage.

"We weren't even asked what we thought!"

"They just used Mandela's name to justify their plans."

Teachers stopped me in the hallways, some angry, others confused.

"Why here?"

"Why now?"

I didn't have answers. I had only instincts—and a deep belief that something sacred had been hijacked.

The announcement wasn't just about naming a school. It was about "co-location." The plan was to house the new Nelson Mandela School for Social Justice within the same building as Boys and Girls High School.

To anyone unfamiliar with the term, co-location might sound benign. Efficient, even. But to those of us who have lived and led within public school systems, it can mean competition, division, and resource conflicts. Two schools under one roof don't always function in harmony. Space is divided. Programs overlap. Identity fractures. And in this case, it felt like our school—the one Mandela himself had chosen to visit—was being used as a prop for political purposes.

I went public. I called the move what I believed it was: opportunistic. I said, on record, that I hadn't been consulted. And when asked if I would resign over it, I didn't mince words. I said I would consider stepping down if the co-location was forced through without genuine dialogue.

That only intensified the firestorm.

Suddenly, I wasn't just a principal. I was a symbol of resistance. News crews showed up at the school gates. Emails flooded my inbox. Some praised my integrity. Others called me stubborn, divisive, a "troublemaker."

Through it all, I stayed focused on our students. I walked the halls, checked in with staff, attended performances, sat in classrooms. I reminded myself of why I had taken the job in the first place: to serve this community, not to serve political pageantry.

But even as I stood firm, I was not immune to reflection.

I asked myself: was I blocking an opportunity for something new and beautiful to grow? Could this new school, if handled right, become a beacon of justice, as its name suggested?

There was a point—weeks after the press conference—when I met quietly with a group of teachers and community leaders. We sat in a circle in the school library, no microphones, no reporters. Just honesty.

One teacher spoke up: "Dr. Gassaway, we understand your anger. We share it. But the kids—what if this school can really make a difference?"

A parent added, "Mandela stood for peace, for transformation. Maybe we can shape this school into something that lives up to that."

Their words didn't erase the pain. But they planted a seed.

I began meeting with DOE officials—not to concede, but to insist that if this school was to bear Mandela's name, then it needed to live up to Mandela's values: justice, inclusion, community. I was particularly concerned about who they would select as the first principal. I wholeheartedly endorsed their selection.

Then, slowly, the conversation shifted. The new school's planning team began listening. They involved community voices. They outlined a curriculum rooted in social justice and equity. They recruited staff who were committed to those ideals. However, they had problems recruiting students. This led to another DOE ploy to "hurt" Boys and Girls High School. The school's chancellor placed a moratorium on BGHS's 2014 entering class. She went further and assigned all of the incoming students (the ones in good academic standing) to Nelson Mandela School for Social Justice.

By June 2014, the Nelson Mandela School for Social Justice opened its doors—right inside the building I had fought to protect. The following is the email (verbatim) that I sent to Chancellor Fariña, which she did not respond to.

Dear Chancellor Fariña,

I am writing to explain why the New York City Department of Education (DOE) policy to place a moratorium on over-the-counter enrollment at Boys and Girls High School (BGHS) may do more harm than good. Ironically, in an effort to redress a flawed policy and practice of discriminately placing overaged and under-credited students at BGHS over the last five to seven years, DOE's current policy of denying BGHS the opportunity to recruit any students is unjustifiable. It is tantamount to phasing out BGHS. Without the ability to recruit, our student register will continue to plummet.

If BGHS is not permitted to recruit now, when will this moratorium be lifted? Will we be denied the opportunity to recruit in October at the High School Fair? If not, why not? If yes, why then and not now? According to Sharon Rencher, it may be unfair to currently enroll any students over the counter this year because BGHS may face closure next year if we do not meet our goals. While this may be a possibility, closure is not a certainty. What is certain is that a blanket moratorium without discretion is unfair to BGHS's effort to recruit students who want to attend BGHS. What is also certain is that BGHS is doomed to fail if we are expected to implement a plan in September 2014 that we have not seen since its first draft in July 2014.

What is not fair is to redirect students who were recruited by BGHS and have expressed interest in attending BGHS to Nelson Mandela School for Social Justice because their enrollment is low.

In order to move forward in good faith, we propose the following. First, provide BGHS with the "District's Redesign Plan." Second, allow BGHS to recruit students until it reaches an agreed-upon student register target—based on our current budget and staffing capacity. Third, allow BGHS to recruit until October 31st for this current school year. I am confident that the New York State Education Department officials will not object to what I am proposing.

In short, DOE must demonstrate its unequivocal support for BGHS. Additional funding without sound policies and practices leads to certain failure. Our children, parents, staff, and community deserve a fighting chance.

I would appreciate your response to my proposal. Thank you.

Sincerely,
Bernard Gassaway

Looking back now, I still wrestle with that time.

I still believe the initial rollout was flawed. I still believe the DOE and the Mayor's office used Mandela's passing as a political opportunity. But I also believe in transformation. In reclaiming a flawed beginning and reshaping it into something powerful. The Nelson Mandela School for Social Justice is not a symbol of surrender. It's a reminder that principled resistance can lead to progress, that sometimes, standing up means staying in.

And I think often about that phone call in my car, about the man who inspired it all. Mandela taught us that resistance without reconciliation is only half the journey. He taught us that protest is only the beginning. Real justice comes when we convert our indignation into creation.

In the end, that's what we did.

The creation of the Mandela School for Social Justice is ultimately the manifestation of turning something from wrong to something right!

We are not makers of history. We are made by history.
                                        —Martin Luther King, Jr.

Race and Leadership

MY own journey with race and leadership began in college. College played a major role in shaping how I dealt with race relations as a school and district leader. I remember during my first year, racial tensions were an undercurrent at LeMoyne College in Syracuse, NY. I recall walking down a path adjacent to the freshmen dormitory and heard an echoed message from an anonymous student: "Niggers pay your own way." I thought this was interesting because I had earlier met with the financial aid officer to take out a loan. I admit I was a recipient of H.E.O.P., where I received financial and academic support for being classified as academically and financially disadvantaged. Other notable racial issues arose during my years at LeMoyne. One stands out more than the rest.

During my junior year at LeMoyne College, a local philanthropist pledged $25,000 for a new library. I was told the donation would support the "Black section" of the library—whatever that meant. As president of the minority cultural society, I was asked to pose for a photo with the donor, standing next to this so-called "Black section."

Later, I met with the college president, Father Frank Haig, and presented him with a list of book titles we wanted. He looked at me and said the donation would actually go toward bricks and mortar. When I reminded him what he had promised, he replied, "You have to understand—sometimes, people have to be used for a higher calling."

That moment changed me. I vowed never to be used like that again. That experience shaped how I've approached every conversation about race ever since— with clarity, courage, and refusal to be silenced.

I remember, as principal, an assistant principal rushed to me in the hallway to report a fight between two students—one from Breezy Point and the other from Redfern. In school code, that meant one student was White and the other Black because of their respective neighborhoods. She feared that if the White student was suspended, we might trigger "White flight." I told her, "Two knuckleheads had a fight. Two knuckleheads will be suspended." I refused to let her racial fears shape disciplinary decisions. By the way—she was White.

While principal of Beach Channel High School, I was anonymously accused of being both racist and anti-Semitic. I didn't respond. I believed then—and still believe—that my actions would speak for themselves. I let my work, not my words, tell the story.

Race is never simple in public institutions. It is always emotional, deeply personal, and often political. But none of that should deter us from confronting it.

Later in my leadership, as superintendent of District 79, I had a principal come to me in distress. One of his teachers had accused him of being racist. I asked him directly, "Are you?" He quickly responded, "No, my sister-in-law is Black." That moment reminded me just how defensive and confused even well-meaning people can be about race. Being called a racist, for many, feels more threatening than confronting racism itself.

Again, while superintendent of District 79, I received a call from Central Office NYCDOE. The chancellor was allegedly concerned that I was hiring "too many Black people." I replied, "I'll stop hiring Black people when Central stops hiring White people." I never received another call like that.

Conclusion

Race and leadership cannot be separated. To lead well in public education is to confront the realities of racism head-on. The responsibility to improve race relations doesn't rest on one race, person, or role. But as educators, we carry a special duty. If we don't challenge racism in our own institutions, who will?

We must change policies and practices, especially in public schools. If we do not, we risk becoming victims of the very racism we failed to confront. To paraphrase George Wallace's infamous words, we may be doomed to "racism today, racism tomorrow, and racism forever."

*The hottest places in hell are reserved for those who, in a
period of moral crisis, maintain their neutrality.*
                                        —Martin Luther King Jr.

CHAMPION OR BYSTANDER?

TEACHERS COLLEGE "ONE LISTEN" EVENT

GOOD evening, President Furman, faculty, staff, students, and guests. I want to thank Chelsey and Paula for inviting me to offer remarks in this One Listen event.

I have decided to frame my remarks on Proverbs 38:1: "Speak up for those who have no voice, for the justice of all who are dispossessed."

Please ponder this question: Are you a champion?

Merriam-Webster's dictionary defines a champion as "someone who fights or speaks publicly in support of a person, belief, or cause"; "a militant advocate or defender"; and "one that does battle for another's rights or honor."

While I agree with these definitions, I would add that champions create cultures of care and do not remain silent when they see injustice. To paraphrase the MTA slogan, if champions see something, they do something. Champions understand that silence is betrayal. They understand what Bill Ayers said about teaching: "Teaching has always been, for me, linked to issues of social justice. I've never considered it a neutral or passive profession."

Were it not for champions in my life, I would not be speaking before you this evening.

As an elementary school student, I do not remember having a champion, other than my mother. I remember being suspended frequently from school for fighting or insubordination.

As a middle school student, my teacher, Mr. Liebowitz, was my champion. He made it possible for me to return to school even after I was arrested for an incident that had occurred outside of school. I was guilty of taking a quarter from another student. For this, I was arrested, and the police took a Polaroid picture of me and placed it on the bulletin board under a sign that read "Gang Members"—even though I was not in a gang.

In high school, my English teacher, Ms. Kleinstein, believed that even students who were classified as at-risk could learn to read Shakespeare's *Romeo and Juliet* and *Macbeth*. Through her care and compassion, she concentrated on convincing me that I could go to college and be successful even when I did not see or believe in my own potential, similar to Jonathan in the podcast Three Miles.

In college, Mr. Carl Thomas, director of H.E.O.P. at LeMoyne College, was my champion. He helped me to understand that I did belong at a Jesuit Institution, even though I was neither White nor Catholic.

My college career almost ended as soon as it began. One day in my first-year English class, the professor said the one word that I never wanted to hear him say: Bernard. You see, he called on me to read aloud. Because I was aware that my education up to that point had been inferior, I was horrified to participate, particularly because I felt like an outsider among all of my Caucasian classmates. This was probably not unlike how the students of University Heights felt when they visited Fieldston. After the professor called my name, my hands trembled, and my knees knocked. In the middle of reading a passage, I made a mistake. Instead of saying "diaphragm," I said, "diagram." As if on cue, the entire class began to laugh, even the professor. I felt so small. This confirmed that I was not supposed to be there. I knew daily, consciously and subconsciously, that I was the only Black student in most of my classes. Instead of reacting violently, as I would have two years prior, I decided to use this experience to work harder. I had something to prove. This was truly a defining moment for me.

Though I considered myself a champion for children, I have learned that even champions need champions.

In 2007, I became a doctoral student at Teachers College (TC). While 95% of my experiences there were positive, I do remember feeling a little intimidated in certain environments within TC. This is ironic because I worked and lived in some of the toughest neighborhoods in New York City. I recall one specific time when I needed to have a form signed—such a simple task. I walked into an office to ask two individuals for help, and they literally berated me. I apparently had unknowingly not followed the established protocol. Fortunately for me, I had a champion at TC. My champion (now my friend) was Ellie Drago-Severson. From the first day of her class, I knew she was caring, compassionate, competent, and very demanding. When I explained to Ellie what I experienced, she did what champions do. She did something! I will leave it at this: I did get the form signed, and I went on to earn my doctorate on May 20, 2015.

As I reflect on the podcast, I wonder if Melanie had any champions at University Heights.

Principal

In 1997, I became the first African American principal at Beach Channel High School in Queens, NY. One day during my fourth year, a student accused a teacher of hitting him. I filed the obligatory report to the Office of Special Investigation. They asked me to investigate the case and submit my findings. I decided to refuse the case and have them investigate it instead. I also insisted that the teacher be removed pending the outcome of the investigation. They complied with my request. After nearly two months, they completed their investigation and found the charges of corporal punishment were substantiated. The superintendent then made the decision to allow the teacher to return to the school. I met with the superintendent and the deputy legal counsel for the Department of Education. I demanded that this teacher not be returned to Beach Channel. In fact, I DID NOT understand why they had NOT terminated the teacher. As they persisted, I informed them if they returned the teacher to my school, I would resign on the spot. They decided not to return the teacher to Beach Channel. It was extremely important for me not to just say something but be prepared to do something.

Regrettably, because of the enormity of the challenges that my students faced, our efforts to champion them were not always successful. I remember when a 17-year-old student requested that I lighten her course load to enable her to come to school later in the day to accommodate her work schedule. I asked her where she worked. She told me that she worked near Grand Central Parkway in Queens. She then explained that she got off work at 5:00 a.m., but she needed to go home and take a shower and get an hour or two of sleep. She explained that she was an escort. Somehow, in her mind, describing her job in this way gave her a level of dignity that did not come with the cruder term *prostitute*. I wish I could tell you that I (we) was instrumental in helping her change her life conditions. That is not the way this story ends. Frankly, I cannot tell you how it ended. I do know that my staff and I used our limited resources and made efforts to support this student, though our efforts were unsuccessful. Perhaps this is how some staff at University Heights felt when they tried to help Melanie.

Teacher of Teachers

I am currently teaching a graduate course in public school finance at another institution. I asked one of my students, a New York City teacher, what she would say to the governor or to members of the New York State Legislature about funding inequities and fixing what she described as a broken school system. She gave a passionate response with several excellent ideas and strategies. I then asked her what was preventing her from delivering her message to them. She responded, "I never thought about it." We may surmise that if she and others remain silent, nothing will change. People often say, "I am only one person. I cannot do anything to change the system." I am reminded of a quote from Margaret Mead: "Never doubt that a small group of thoughtful, committed citizens can change the world; indeed, it's the only thing that ever has."

In closing, when I listened to the podcast, I did not think of social justice; rather, I thought of the effects of injustice. When I think of injustice, I can hear it, see it, feel it, taste it, and smell it. In other words, it is palpable. I think of the high suspension rates among African American boys, the school-to-prison pipeline, homelessness, illiteracy, poverty, racism, violence, gaps in all categories, and inferior education. This describes the experiences of University Heights students and many of my students; in fact, it also describes my own experiences.

Furthermore, when I think of social injustice, I ask myself what responsibility, if any, an institution has for addressing social justice challenges, first within the institution itself and second within the larger community. What role, if any, should, for example, TC play in influencing, shaping, and (when necessary) correcting the urban educational discourse? Does TC have a moral responsibility to not only say something but *do* something?

The answer lies in this quote from Helen Keller: "Until the great mass of the people shall be filled with the sense of responsibility for each other's welfare, social justice can never be attained."

So, I ask, are you willing to speak up for those who have no voice? Are you willing to be a champion?

Thank you!

PART II

LEADERSHIP IN PRACTICE

I don't think we can do a good enough job providing good teachers for our schools.

—Frank Mickens

NOBODY MESSES WITH
MY KIDS

I remember being interviewed by Frank Mickens for a teaching position at Boys and Girls High School in 1988. Two things in particular stand out from that meeting. First, he asked me if I was married. I recall being taken aback. I thought a prospective employer wasn't allowed to ask that kind of question. Nevertheless, I answered yes. What happened next stunned me. Mickens slammed his fist on the table and screamed, "Nobody messes with my kids."

I thought he was crazy. Who was this man who shouted at a job candidate in the middle of an interview, invoking a kind of protectionist fury I had never witnessed in a school leader? I would later come to understand. Not immediately, but gradually—over the course of my career as an assistant principal, then principal, and eventually as a superintendent—I began to grasp the full meaning of Mickens' proclamation.

His words were not just rhetorical flourishes or performative bluster. They were a creed, a boundary line, a personal code of ethics drawn in bold letters. "Nobody messes with my kids" meant there was no higher priority than the physical, emotional, and intellectual protection of children. It meant no adult ego, no political agenda, no union contract, no bureaucratic directive would supersede the obligation to care for and shield young people. Mickens understood that in a world designed to erode the possibilities for Black and Brown children—especially in urban public schools—protection wasn't a passive duty. It required confrontation. Resistance. Edge.

Throughout my leadership tenure, I came to understand, in the broadest sense, what Mickens meant. I embraced his mantra with fervor. It became a guiding light for my leadership. It shaped how I walked through the hallways, how I spoke to teachers and parents, how I crafted policies, and how I made decisions.

As I reflect on my career, I cannot recall a time when I did not have to fight for children. There was never a moment when doing the right thing came without resistance. I wasn't naïve. I entered school administration with the clear intention of improving conditions for children—especially those who had been historically underserved and systemically neglected. My philosophy from the beginning was simple: It's all about the kids.

But experience added layers to that simplicity. Over time, I realized it was also about the adults who were tasked with serving and protecting those kids. Teachers, counselors, deans, paraprofessionals, cafeteria workers, security guards—these adults held enormous power over the everyday lives of children. When they showed up with love, belief, and commitment, kids thrived. But when they showed up bitter, entitled, indifferent, or overwhelmed, kids were harmed. And I had to protect children not only from the world outside, but also from the adults inside the school building.

What I did not expect—what shook me to my core—was the realization that I would have to protect children from the very system that claimed to protect them, a system of education that spoke the language of equity, achievement, and inclusion—but too often trafficked in practices of exclusion, punishment, degradation, and failure.

I confronted physical violence—fights among students—incidents that could have been prevented with better supervision, better relationships, better leadership.

I confronted psychological violence: teachers who belittled students with sarcasm and low expectations, administrators who punished children for being poor, for being late, for being traumatized.

I confronted academic violence: curricula devoid of cultural relevance, schools that expected children to perform without being taught, testing regimes that sorted and labeled kids without ever building them up.

And I confronted character assassination—against me, against other leaders, and sometimes even against the children themselves, all because we dared to disrupt the status quo.

In all these moments, my job was to fight, to be the barrier between harm and hope, to take the hit if necessary.

At some point—after serving as teacher, assistant principal, principal, and then superintendent—I reached a painful conclusion: the system was not broken. It was designed to fail children. If education were a game, the outcome would be fixed. Team Children was meant to lose.

To stay in the fight, I had to shift my mindset. I adopted what I now describe as a "Malcolm X approach"—win by any means necessary. That didn't mean reckless rebellion. It meant strategic defiance. It meant I was no longer afraid of losing my job. If standing up for children cost me my title or my paycheck, so be it.

What many failed to realize is that when I fought for children, I wasn't just fighting for them—I was fighting for myself. I saw my younger self in every student who walked through those doors.

Every chapter in this book is a testament to that kind of leadership—bold, courageous, and rooted in love. These stories aren't just anecdotes. They are evidence. They are battle scars and survival notes. They are blueprints for those who dare to lead from the edge.

When I taught educational leadership at the College of Saint Rose, I would often pose a question to my graduate students: "What is your price?" In other words, "How much will it cost for you to stop protecting children?" That question was not abstract. The system they were seeking to advance in would one day force them to answer it.

Would they remain silent in the face of a racist policy because their supervisor said it was district-wide?

Would they look the other way when a beloved teacher shamed a student, just to avoid conflict with the union?

Would they sign off on budget cuts that devastated student support services, just to keep their job secure?

At some point, every leader reaches that edge, the point where they must decide whether to lean in or back away. I decided long ago that I didn't have a price. You couldn't buy my silence with a promotion or fear of losing my job. You couldn't purchase my complicity with a title.

My love for children—real love, not performative love—could not be compromised. And that love shaped my philosophy, my posture, and my practice.

It made me a protector.

It made me a disruptor.

It made me a truth-teller.

It made me dangerous to systems of complacency.

And it made me a servant of something greater than any institution.

That's what edge leadership is.

Frank Mickens understood that. He modeled it before I had language for it. And now, decades later, I understand why he slammed his fist on that table and said what he said.

"Nobody messes with my kids."

All that I am, or ever hope to be, I owe to my angel mother.

—Abraham Lincoln

FULL-CIRCLE MOMENT: A MOTHER'S LOVE

I remember when I was in the seventh grade, a teacher slapped me. I was shocked. I went home and told my mother. She brought me back to the school, and the assistant principal explained what had happened. The teacher had a brace on his thumb. For some reason that I don't recall, I pulled his thumb back, causing him excruciating pain. I remember seeing stars after his open hand made contact with my face.

Immediately after learning the full story, my mother slapped me—in front of the teacher and the assistant principal.

I also remember being accused of spraying a fire extinguisher in the schoolyard. This time, my mother couldn't make it to the school, so she sent my older sister. She was a fierce advocate. She said, "There's no way he did what you're accusing him of." I was proud to have her in my corner. Years later—long after my time as a public school student—I confessed to her: I did spray the fire extinguisher. Don't ask me why.

I can't even count how many times I was suspended from school—it happened a lot. The final incident that got me kicked out of Lefferts Junior High School was when I set a bulletin board on fire. Apparently, someone had seen me jump over the fence on the Empire Boulevard exit.

Throughout all my turbulent years as a wayward youth, my mother hung in there as long as she could. She dutifully showed up for parent-teacher nights—and more frequently, for disciplinary hearings. Eventually, she got to a point where she'd say, "Before you tell me what he did, I already know he did it." She was right. One of my biggest regrets in life is putting my mother through so much hell—especially the embarrassment.

Fast forward to my time as principal at Boys and Girls High School. One day, from my office, I heard a woman screaming at the top of her lungs. I could only make out profanity. A dean came to my office and said, "There's a crazy parent at the main entrance, and school safety is about to arrest her." I told him, "Bring her to my office." He looked at me and asked, "Are you sure?" I said yes.

The parent—still screaming—was brought to my conference room by the dean and a school safety agent. I asked them to leave me alone with the parent and her son. The dean hesitated, but I assured him I was good.

The parent directed her anger and frustration at me. I just sat there and listened as she cursed me out. At some point—what felt like an eternity—she yelled, "What are you looking at?" I said, "You. You're talking to me." Then I turned to her son, who seemed to be enjoying the show. I said, "See what you're doing to your mother?"

That shifted her attention. She turned to him and said, "I had to cancel my appointment to look at an apartment, and you made me come all the way from the Bronx. You know today is my birthday!"

I said, "Happy birthday, Ma."

She calmed down, and we were able to talk about her son's behavior. Honestly, I don't remember what became of him. But when she mentioned her appointment and that she had come from the Bronx, I knew—through experience—that she and her children were living in a shelter.

In so many ways, I couldn't help but think about my own mother, coming to school because of my misbehavior. I was reminded of the time we were homeless and lived at the Granada Hotel (a shelter) in downtown Brooklyn, before my mother found an apartment on Dumont and Warwick in East New York.

As a teacher, assistant principal, principal, and superintendent, I experienced countless full-circle moments. I've always been clear about my why. I've been driven by memories of my mother, who never got to see me become an educator before she died.

I've wanted to reach boys—especially boys—before they went delinquent. I didn't want any mother to go through what mine did. During my days of running the streets, cutting school, and getting arrested, somehow, I was spared. And I believe I was spared for a reason—to do the work I was doing.

It is my fervent belief that our schools can work if given an atmosphere that promotes academic excellence, school pride and sense of purpose.

—Frank Mickens

Mickens Model: Mentorship

FRANK Mickens' leadership had a profound impact on my own journey as an educator and leader. I had the good fortune of witnessing his greatness up close and personal. Around 1990, I sat on stage at Boys and Girls High School during an awards ceremony, watching him command the auditorium with a fierce yet loving intensity. That moment would stay with me for the rest of my life. The way he celebrated student achievement and held our young people—particularly our young Black boys— to high standards was nothing short of inspiring. Later, I would model my own awards ceremonies on his blueprint, always mindful of how public acknowledgment could shape identity, dignity, and direction.

At that same ceremony, I vividly remember Mickens introducing the formation of a new student group: The Sophisticated Gents. He envisioned a cadre of young men who dressed well, carried themselves with pride, and were exposed to what it meant to be honorable and respectable young Black men. It wasn't just about image—it was about values, identity, and collective responsibility. That seed Mickens planted took root in me and countless others.

Years later, I joined an organization called

C.L.I.M.B.—Commitment to the Longevity and Improvement of Male Blacks. C.L.I.M.B. was a volunteer-run, not-for-profit group serving Black boys primarily from South Jamaica and Brooklyn. We met every Saturday to mentor these young boys through workshops, group discussions, and trips. One of our most impactful traditions was the upstate retreats to Camp Sunrise. These experiences gave boys a chance to disconnect from the pressures of the neighborhood and connect more deeply with one another—and with us. They found safe space and brotherhood in those woods.

Interestingly, when I later became principal of Boys and Girls High School, I brought that tradition full circle. Along with other dedicated male staff, I began taking our male students to Camp Sunrise as well. It was symbolic—a return to the values instilled by Mickens, reimagined for a new generation. We wanted to offer our boys not just a break from their daily struggles, but also an entryway into reflection, community, and hope.

That wasn't the only initiative inspired by my commitment to Black male mentorship. For over 25 years now, I have served as Chairman of the Board of a not-for-profit organization called R.I.S.E.—Recreational Inner-City Sports and Education. R.I.S.E. continues to provide young people with access to sports, academic support, and mentorship. What I've learned over the decades is that real change doesn't always come from a grand reform plan. Sometimes, it emerges from consistent presence, patient listening, and purposeful programming.

One of the programs I am most proud of from my time at Boys and Girls High School was Boys II Men Night. The idea was simple but powerful. We recruited staff—especially male role models—to volunteer their time for a school sleepover. The catch: no one actually slept. Instead, we ran workshops, allowed the boys to play basketball, compete in video games, and even play a game called "Man Hunt." We cooked real food—provided snacks—and provided enough sustenance and conversation to keep everyone going all night.

The results were profound. Boys who wouldn't normally even acknowledge each other in the hallway found themselves laughing, learning, and bonding across divides. Boys II Men Night broke barriers. It built brotherhood. It helped students see themselves and each other differently. And most importantly, it reminded them that they mattered—to us and to one another.

All of these efforts preceded President Barack Obama's My Brother's Keeper Initiative. Long before it became a national conversation, we had already taken action. We didn't wait for permission or policy shifts. We acted on principle, urgency, and love.

In my article "Brainwash Black Boys to Brilliance," I called out the painful truth: "Choose any major urban city and the data on Black boys is the same: Negative." The odds, for too many of our boys, are tragically predictable. One Harvard professor noted that "about two-thirds of African-American men with low levels of schooling will go to prison in their lifetime."

Beyond just incarceration and poverty, the real danger lies in the narratives. "Images of Black boys as being delinquent and defiant, wayward and worthless... stubborn and stupid, immature and incapable," flood our media and seep into the minds of our youth—and those who educate them. "As these stereotypes are accepted, it becomes easier for people to literally and metaphorically destroy and kill Black boys with apathy or impunity."

But I offer hope. In that same article, I laid out seven strategies to rewrite this narrative—to indoctrinate Black boys with their brilliance. "Train Black boys in the community to embrace their brilliance... Teach Black boys to affirm their brilliance... Provide Black boys with evidence of their brilliance." These are not just strategies—they are imperatives.

Our boys must be surrounded by affirmations, opportunities, and examples. We must, as I wrote, "do whatever is necessary to protect and nurture Black boys so they can grow to become healthy Black men."

Frank Mickens modeled that kind of leadership—intentional, loving, demanding, and transformational. I've tried to honor that model in every role I've held, every program I've built, and every boy I've mentored, because the work is not about us. It's about what—and who—comes next.

You cannot serve two masters. You cannot serve children and remain silent while they are being hurt under your watch.

—Bernard Gassaway

COST OF ADVOCACY: BECOMING A TARGET FOR FIGHTING FOR CHILDREN

WHEN you fight for children, you become a target. When you seek to change the culture of a school with a sense of urgency, you become a target. When you focus on instruction and give constructive feedback, you become a target. One way for malcontent staff to take you out is to report false allegations anonymously.

I have been the subject of numerous allegations—mainly based on financial embezzlement. My first embezzlement allegation occurred when I was principal at Beach Channel High School. I remember walking out of my office and seeing an Office of Special Investigator (OSI) staff member, Bob Smalls. I knew him because I had filed reports with his office on several occasions for teacher misconduct, usually involving inappropriate relations with students (fortunately, I did not have many of these). I asked Bob, "So what brings you here today?" He said, "You." He appeared to be uncomfortable, as if he did not believe the allegation—which was that I was spending school money for personal reasons, along with the Parent-Teacher Association president—a person who was beyond reproach. Bob asked if I wanted a union representative present at the interview. I said no. I knew the reason for the allegation and knew it was not true. I always believed and espoused: if you were clean, they could not find any dirt. This particular allegation was immediately unfounded.

Another allegation, again anonymous, was that I spent most of my day sitting in my assistant principal's office talking about sex and smoking weed. I was informed by one of the assistant superintendents of this allegation. I simply responded, "I don't smoke weed—anymore!"

Another allegation was filed when I was at Boys and Girls High School—embezzlement again. This time, I was accused of writing checks from the general school fund. The investigator came from the Special Commissioner of Investigation's office—an independent mayoral office. The investigator requested copies of checks dated back three years. Again, I was asked if I wanted union representation. Again, I declined. I do advise aspiring and current school leaders to have representation present. I simply did not care; again, I knew I was not guilty. If anything, I was guilty of using my own money to support students and families.

Another allegation filed with OSI was that I hired a substitute teacher to cover a physical education vacancy long-term. This was true; however, I did not understand why this was an OSI case. I had served as a long-term

physical education teacher at I.S. 59 in Springfield
Gardens, NY, for two years. Apparently, there was some
rule that was never enforced about a physical education
vacancy being covered by a non-licensed teacher. I did
have a union representative with me in this case, though
it did not help. She had apparently done no "homework"
about my case before showing up. She asked me before the
interview what the case was about. I asked the investigator
why this allegation was being handled by OSI and not
the superintendent's office. She declined to answer. It
was clearly a personnel matter. Again, I understand I
had a target on my back because of my years of public
advocacy. I was never worried about the outcome of the
case because, frankly, I did not care. I understand my
purpose—I approached this work like I was on a mission.

My final interaction with OSI did not involve an
allegation against me. One day, an OSI investigator
came to my office to interview a student about a case
that occurred when the student was in middle school, a
year prior to enrolling in Boys and Girls High School.
I asked the investigator if the case involved the student's
parents. He said no. I then said I would call the parent to
get her approval for the interview, which was generally my
practice. I know I would not want my child interviewed
without my knowledge. The investigator told me he did
not need approval because he worked for NYCDOE. I
told him it was my practice to inform parents and get
their approval—again, he insisted that he did not need
their approval. I thought to myself, he would not be so

aggressive if he were in a White, affluent, or middle-class school. I demanded the same treatment for my students.

The investigator thought he was smart and told me that I had the authority to approve the interview because of in loco parentis. I said, "Since I am the parent, you cannot interview the student." He was infuriated. After I told him to leave the building, he notified my superintendent, who was actually scheduled to be at my school for a meeting in a couple of hours. When she showed up, the investigator was with her. She told me to let him interview the student. I again, emphatically, said no! Shortly after, I received a call from a lawyer from the Chancellor's Office, along with the director of OSI. The exchange was heated. All I remember is that the investigator left the building without interviewing the student. I could not help thinking about the racial implications of this case.

I have been sued on several occasions, which is part of the public record. In each case, I stood up for what I believed was right—for students. My last lawsuit was most painful because I had already resigned from NYCDOE. Unbeknownst to me, a case of harassment and age discrimination had been filed against me for removing a teacher who had allegedly verbally abused a student. I was unaware of the case until a lawyer from the NYC Corporation Counsel contacted me. He claimed not to have my contact information, and if he had not reached me that day, the case would move forward without me, and likely I would have received a summary judgment not in my favor for failure to comply. I thought: how could I comply if I was not aware of the case? It was reported to the courts that I was served two or three years earlier at an address I had moved from. Ultimately, the case was ruled in my favor.

Upon reflection, I realize that in all of my battles with school officials and teachers, I could have avoided them by just looking the other way. While I make no claim to being a perfect human being, I do stand on the truth that when children were in harm's way, I did my best to protect them—knowing that there would be a price for me to pay. I have all of my receipts!

A vision without a strategy remains an illusion.

—Lee G. Bolman

VISION: SEE IT, BELIEVE IT, ACHIEVE IT

I remember several students approaching me in the hallway asking about the possibility of having a courtroom in our school. Beach Channel, at the time, was divided into houses, and one of the houses was the law program. Obviously, I could not build a courtroom on demand, but the seed was planted.

While serving as principal, I was recruited by a friend to serve on the Queens District Attorney African Advisory Council. This was a great way for me to meet various public officials and community leaders. It was through this experience that I began to grow into my role as a community leader. Each month, a special guest would be invited to the council meetings to share insights on a topic of interest. One notable leader was NYPD Queens South Chief Joseph Fox. After his presentation, I introduced myself to him and invited him to visit the school. We scheduled the meeting, and his visit went very well. He said, "Please let me know if you need any of the resources at my disposal." We went on to collaborate on other community activities, most notably the Thanksgiving Day Senior Dinner.

I learned a great deal from serving on this council.

Thanks to Jesse Sligh and District Attorney Richard Brown, the vision for a school courtroom began to take shape.

One day, the idea struck me to call Mr. Sligh to ask if he had any old courtroom furniture that I could use to start a courtroom at the school. Frankly, I was hoping for a bench. As fortune would have it, he informed me that a courtroom was being renovated, and we could have all of the furniture—if we could dismantle and transport it to the school. I approached one of our teachers, a skilled carpenter, who agreed to dismantle the courtroom.

I told Mr. Sligh we would need help with transportation. As luck would have it, his office had a truck that had been seized in a drug case. If we could find a driver, we could use it. We made it happen.

Once we got the furniture to the school, the next step was preparing the room. We identified three obsolete shops that were adjacent to one another. I envisioned these spaces as the future home of the courtroom. Some people did not see the vision because the rooms were divided by walls. But I envisioned the walls being knocked down.

I contacted a gentleman at the School Construction Authority and invited him to visit the space and hear our vision. As fortune would have it, his daughter was in law school, so he basically adopted the project. It became personal for him. It also became personal for some of my staff, who volunteered to make a robe for the student judge. The carpenter-teacher donated his skills and engaged students in the project.

This is how The Rockaway WAVE (January 15, 2000) recorded the significance of the project:

Students and faculty of Beach Channel High School played host to community leaders at the opening of the school's new Law Center on Wednesday, January 12. The ribbon-cutting ceremony of the Beach Channel High School Law Center was attended by more than 100 people, including Queens District Attorney Richard Brown, Judge Jean Fox, Assistant Chief Joseph Fox of Patrol Borough Queens South, Captain Gary Scirica of the 100th Precinct, Congressman Gregory Meeks, Assemblywoman Audrey Pheffer, and Queens High School Superintendent John Lee.

The Law Center houses many activities related to Beach Channel's new Law Institute, which began offering courses in February. The facility is an actual courtroom dismantled and transported from a Queens County courthouse. It was reassembled and refurbished by the students of Robert Schropp, a teacher at Beach Channel. The courtroom includes a judge's chamber, jury room, and observation classroom, which supports a four-year, law-oriented program for students.

"This dream of mine is beginning to come true," I said during the ceremony. "We want to link our excellent oceanography and environmental science program with courses dealing with legal issues related to those areas. Our collaboration with Southampton College and its nationally recognized program in marine and environmental science will help guide us in planning and implementing quality courses."

Howard Galin, a social studies teacher for 26 years with a long and accomplished history at Beach Channel, oversaw the Law Institute. "Educated students make the best citizens," he said, explaining that students in the Law Institute would complete state-mandated social studies courses, plus additional courses in international, federal, state, and consumer law.

Beginning in the fall of 2000, students from throughout the city had the opportunity to apply for admission to the Beach Channel Law Institute Program.

I was honored to be credited by those who attended the ceremony for having the vision to move such an ambitious project forward. "You come to Beach Channel High School and believe we have a strong future…in the right direction," said Assemblywoman Audrey Pheffer.

"There are so many people who made this facility a reality," I added. "Richard Brown made things materialize, and John Pellegrano of School Facilities put them together. It is up to us to make it all a part of realizing our students' dreams."

Success is not measured by what you accomplish, but by the opposition you have encountered, and the courage with which you have maintained the struggle against overwhelming odds.

—Orison Swett Marden

Vote of No Confidence: Fight or Flight

I began my principalship at Boys and Girls High School in July of 2009. From the outset, I felt both the weight of responsibility and the call of purpose. Upon returning to the school—where I had once served as a teacher from 1988 to 1991—I crossed paths with a familiar face. I saw a teacher I had worked with decades earlier and greeted him warmly, saying, "What's up? When you get a moment, I would love to catch up with you about what's happening at BGHS." I meant it with sincere intentions.

That same evening, I received a call from the teachers' union representative. He said a teacher claimed I was harassing him. That was the moment I knew—clear as day—what I was walking into. From that day forward, I understood the environment I was in and adjusted accordingly. I became guarded, not out of fear, but out of wisdom.

A Mission, Not Just a Job

Before taking the helm at BGHS, I had served in multiple leadership roles: teacher, assistant principal,

principal of Beach Channel High School, and superintendent of District 79 in NYC. I was not stepping into the unknown—I was stepping into the fire with full knowledge of the terrain and the tools to withstand the heat.

What I encountered almost immediately was disorder—student discipline issues, teacher resistance, and, in many cases, a lack of meaningful leadership from the assistant principal ranks. Not all were resistant, but the status quo was deeply entrenched. I came into the building with a sense of urgency. And I made that clear in one of my first meetings—with Chancellor Joel Klein.

I asked Chancellor Klein for five things:

1. Do not designate BGHS as an "Impact School" (which would bring in NYPD to patrol hallways).
2. Allow me to revamp the school's security staff.
3. Permit me to replace certain assistant principals.
4. Refrain from installing metal detectors.
5. Appoint me as a master principal (with a $25,000 additional salary).

He approved all but the last request, which I didn't consider a deal-breaker. My mission was bigger than money and a title.

Crisis and Immediate Action

Shortly after I took office, in August 2009, a violent incident occurred—two girls on the track team got into a fight in the locker room. One slashed the other's face with a razor blade. That incident changed everything. Despite my earlier efforts to avoid scanning, I could not argue against the implementation of metal detectors. Student safety trumped every ideal.

I met with the president of the supervisors' union shortly thereafter to inform him of my plans to remove certain assistant principals. While he did not support my decision, he also did not interfere. That, for me, was enough.

By the end of the second year, we had discipline under control, thanks to the efforts of many dedicated staff members. During the first year, I recall a major altercation that resembled a riot. My response? I removed overaged, under-credited students who were not serious about education and only came to disrupt the environment. According to DOE guidelines, those students may have remained in school indefinitely. But I refused to sacrifice the safety of many for the comfort of a few.

Confronting the Real Challenge: Instruction

While discipline was the most visible problem, the root cause of our academic decline was poor instruction. This realization brought me into direct conflict with the teachers' union. If we wanted to shift school culture, it had to begin in the classroom. The problem? In many classrooms, very little teaching—or learning—was actually happening.

The union rep once approached me and said the teachers would support me—and even give me a higher rating on the school's report—under one condition: slow down on observing and evaluating teachers' lessons. I declined. I would not trade integrity for optics.

As a result, they continued to rate my leadership poorly. Then came the moment I'll never forget—my second year, word reached me that the teachers had gathered in the library to draft a resolution of no confidence in my leadership. I didn't see the letter at the time, and I don't believe it was ever formally submitted. But years later, I came across a copy. Here it is:

Resolution of the Staff of Boys and Girls High School

June 22, 2011

    A.   *Whereas the principal has waged a slanderous and libelous public media campaign against the teachers of Boys and Girls High School, labeling them "incompetent," "unmotivated," and harmful to children in several national and local media outlets;*

B. *Whereas the principal and his administrative
    team have used the observation process for punitive
    rather than developmental purposes of training
    teachers and improving instruction;*

C. *Whereas the principal has removed key
    instructional leaders in major disciplines (math,
    social studies, special education and foreign
    language) and replaced them with less experienced
    and/or qualified substitutes that are incapable of
    offering teachers developmental support to improve
    instruction in their discipline;*

D. *Whereas the principal has fostered an unsafe
    teaching and learning environment by failing
    to effectively address student violations of the
    Discipline Code and/or under-reporting such
    violations;*

E. *Whereas the principal has created conditions
    for the wholesale academic failure of students
    by: authorizing and/or supervising the
    misprogramming of special education students
    into "mainstream" and "oversized" classes despite
    the recommendations of their teachers and/or
    specifications of their IEP; enacting a misguided
    and poorly executed "A/B Day" program; denying
    students preparation for Regents exams by
    terminating Regents Review classes and failing
    to program them for classes that would provide
    preparation for Regents exams;*

F. *Whereas the principal has quantitatively demonstrated an inability to push Regents performance, graduation rates and attendance in a significantly positive direction in the past two years despite being offered every degree of support from the New York City Department of Education, the State Education Department and local community organizations;*

G. *Whereas the principal has accepted no responsibility for the school's academic performance for the past two years and has instead exclusively blamed teachers for the school's failure, creating a hostile and counterproductive tone;*

H. *Whereas the principal has unilaterally refused to accept federal "Restart" funding to provide needed professional development to teachers, he claims lack of instructional skill while also failing to appoint experienced and qualified assistant principals to lead them, leaving teachers no opportunity for instructional growth;*

I. *Whereas the principal has yet to fully and clearly articulate his "vision" for the future of Boys and Girls High School.*

    We, the undersigned teachers of Boys and Girls High School, resolve to withdraw our confidence in the ability of Mr. Gassaway to lead our school during this difficult time and request that the UFT work with the NYC DOE to find a more suitable

> *and effective leader in the hopes of moving our*
> *school towards success rather than continued blame*
> *of teachers, failure and closure.*

A Necessary Confrontation

To be completely honest, I was guilty of nearly everything in that resolution.

Yes, I removed assistant principals who had become part of the problem.

Yes, I spoke critically of a system that protected incompetence.

Yes, I challenged instructional mediocrity.

Yes, I made people uncomfortable.

But everything I did was in service of the students. The status quo could not continue—not on my watch.

What I came to realize is that in some schools, a loud minority of influential teachers can drive the entire building's culture. At BGHS, many teachers wanted improvement and supported my efforts quietly. But the louder voices resisted change. They preferred the chaos. It distracted from the real work of instruction and learning.

The Culture of Conflict Avoidance

There was also a deeply embedded culture of conflict avoidance. I remember asking several assistant principals to conduct classroom observations. They refused. One even admitted, "We were told by the prior principal not to write unsatisfactory observations—too many griev-ances." The playbook was: "Don't see anything. Don't say anything." That was the shield of complacency. I broke that shield.

My leadership was not about keeping the peace. It was about creating the conditions for learning, even if that meant walking through fire to get there.

Conclusion: No Confidence, Full Commitment

So yes, the staff passed a vote of no confidence. But I took it not as an insult, but as confirmation: I was doing my job. I was disrupting the patterns of dysfunction that had kept students from reaching their potential for far too long.

Change is not welcomed by everyone. It is often mischaracterized. It is resisted. And it is painful. But it is necessary. I did not come to BGHS to be liked. I came to lead.

And lead I did.

Focus and determination beat brains and intellect every time.

—Mark Sanborn

LEADERSHIP DECISIONS: STRATEGIC ADVOCACY

I remember when I served as a superintendent, principals in my district were not paid on par with traditional high school principals. At some point in the history of the supervisors' union salary negotiations, a decision was made that alternative school principals were not worthy of parity. One argument likely rested on the fact that alternative schools had smaller student enrollment.

This argument held until Mayor Michael Bloomberg began his small schools movement. He believed that many of the traditional, larger schools were failing hundreds of thousands of students, in part due to their size, which made them unmanageable. In some ways, I agreed with him. Some small schools began with as few as 50 students and were capped at around 300. I noted that principals of these small schools received the same salaries as traditional high school principals.

This led me to reinitiate the principal parity conversation, a fight that had begun under my two predecessors. As with most of my efforts, I faced resistance. My strategy was bold, focused, and relationship-driven. I began planting seeds with individuals who could help. I spoke with my immediate supervisor, Dr. Lester Young,

Jr. Once he was on board, I moved forward. I met with Dan Weisberg, who oversaw labor relations for the NYC DOE. He outlined what needed to happen to achieve parity. I am convinced parity would not have been possible without his guidance and covert support.

During that time, a doctoral classmate of mine from Teachers College was a deputy chancellor at the DOE. Eventually, I was told that the New York City Council would need to approve or sign off on principal parity. As luck would have it, DOE leadership was asked to present before the council on an unrelated matter. I believe I was asked to attend, along with Joyce R. Coppin and Jean-Claude Brizard, to ensure Black representation.

Initially, I refused to attend. I understood race politics, and I knew my presence was requested solely because I was Black. The Mayor's Office was attuned to race optics—so was I. I agreed to attend only on one condition—that I could raise the issue of principal parity. I was told no. I refused to go. A day or two before the hearing, I was told I could raise the issue only if council members brought up funding.

The meeting was chaired by Council Member Eva Moskowitz, a strong and effective voice. I sat silently until I heard someone mention funding. That's when I raised my hand. Once acknowledged, I explained the inequity of the situation. No decision was made that day, but the president of the Council of Supervisors and Administrators told me it was a bad idea to raise the issue. In hindsight, it was probably because I crossed an invisible line related to labor negotiations. I ignored him.

Several months after the hearing, Chancellor Joel Klein approved principal parity, including a measured amount of back pay.

After students with special needs repeatedly failed the Regents Competency Test, I zeroed in on the special education teachers. I asked each what they taught. Almost without fail, they said "special education." I had to remind them that special education is not a subject; it is a service. This, I surmised, was the root of the problem.

I scheduled a meeting with the NYC DOE Human Resources team, including Executive Director Larry Becker and about 10 others. I opened by stating I wanted to excess all 12 generalist special education teachers. Someone objected. Mr. Becker asked her to hear me out. I proposed replacing them with teachers who had content specialties.

Mr. Becker confirmed that, according to the rules, I could proceed. I learned a valuable lesson: know the rules before you play the game. Ultimately, I negotiated to excess six teachers and hired two guidance counselors—both of whom continue to do great work.

As a leader, you cannot avoid making difficult decisions. I decided early on that I would fight to protect children at all costs. Interestingly, while some of my battles were public, most of my victories came behind closed doors. When you fight publicly, people dig in—it becomes harder to negotiate.

I remember when it was all over the papers that the Panel for Educational Policy was scheduled to vote on closing Boys and Girls High School. I knew that if the vote took place, the public pressure would push members to support closure. Despite local and state support, it likely wouldn't be enough to sway the powerful Mayor Bloomberg.

Unbeknownst to my political allies, I called Chancellor Dennis Walcott and requested a meeting. He agreed. We met about a week before the vote at the U.S.A. Diner in Queens. We talked for about an hour—55 minutes of that time was spent sharing personal stories. Then Walcott asked, "So what are we going to do about Boys and Girls High School?" I told him I needed more time.

The next day, the school was removed from the list of closures. Until now, few people have heard this story. Had I gone public and rallied the troops, Boys and Girls High School would be closed today. I thank Chancellor Walcott for his decision.

The quality of your life is built on the quality of your decisions.

—Wesam Fawzi

The quality of your leadership is built on the quality of your decisions.

—Bernard Gassaway

DECISION: EXECUTE

DECISION-MAKING is the lifeline of leading on the edge. Indecision is not a viable option. For leaders, making decisions is like breathing or walking—you do it so often that you rarely stop to think about the mechanics.

I shudder to think about some of the most critical decisions I made during my tenure as a leader in the New York City Department of Education. I remember my first bomb threat as a principal as if it were yesterday. We had approximately 2,600 students on register. My secretary informed me of the call, which was how the threat was communicated. I called the police and then the superintendent, in that order. I asked the superintendent what I should do. He said it was my call since I was on-site. I needed more guidance, but that's all I got. When the police arrived, I decided to evacuate the building.

Since the caller did not identify a specific location, the entire building had to be searched before we could return. I remember it being a nice day, weather-wise. About 30 minutes into our evacuation, the police informed me that the bomb-sniffing dog was on a call in the Bronx. I remember thinking—there's only one dog? We did not have a designated location to relocate the students, so we remained outside the school, about two blocks away.

After nearly an hour of waiting, the students began to disperse on their own. It was unreasonable to expect teachers to keep them contained. Students scattered. It was close to noon, and we normally dismissed at 2:30 p.m.

The next day, I was informed that the students had ransacked the local Waldbaum supermarket.

Within days of receiving the first bomb threat, we received another. I followed the same protocol and notified the police. The fire department also showed up. I was conflicted about whether to evacuate, given what had happened previously. I asked the supervising fireman if I should evacuate. He initially said it was my call, then added, "If I were you…" I immediately snapped back, "You're not me." In hindsight, I know I reacted sharply because of the gravity of the situation. I decided not to evacuate the building. In fact, I never evacuated a school again after that first time. I relied on judgment in each case. As of today, I have a perfect track record—thank God. Each decision was made with the utmost level of discernment.

Immediately following 9/11, the number of bomb threats increased. This was an international phenomenon.

I remember on 9/11 being under an enormous amount of stress. Shortly after the planes hit the Twin Towers, parents and guardians descended on the school. One parent came to pick up her child and offered to take a neighbor's child as well. I decided against this. Fortunately, in the chaos, I made the right decision. Within 10–25 minutes, the neighbor arrived to pick up her child. I often think about what would have happened if I had released that student to someone other than their guardian.

My lesson from this incident was clear: as a leader, you must be the eye of the storm. Decisions must be made calmly and deliberately. Once you go through the process, make a decision and live with it—whether it proves right or wrong.

One of the most critical decisions I ever made was quitting my first assistant principal job after only one day. I had been hired by the principal of Murray Bertram High School in Manhattan, who was also my professor at Baruch College. At the end of the course, she offered me the position of assistant principal of organization. I must have impressed her as a student.

I reported on the opening day of the school year, the last week in August. I was anxious, as this was my first role as an assistant principal. I had no idea what the specific duties entailed, but I wanted the job and figured I could learn on the go. My initial shock came when I was given a large ring with at least 100 keys. Seeing them immediately stressed me out. After meeting with the principal, the assistant principal of guidance informed me that I would also be responsible for security—a role she had held prior to my arrival. This heightened my anxiety. I never wanted anything to do with security, likely because, as a student, I was the dean's worst nightmare. Somehow, I made it through the day, but I remember nothing of it beyond the keys and the added responsibility.

As I sat on the J-train heading home to Jamaica, Queens, I told myself one of two things would happen: I would either get divorced or have a heart attack from the stress of the job—or both. I called my college mentor, Herb Coleman, who advised me to call the principal and rescind my acceptance. I did so, and the principal graciously accepted my decision. I felt an immediate relief unlike anything I had experienced before or since.

Another major decision was closing the New Beginning sites. Someone in DOE leadership had developed the idea of having targeted schools remove their most violent and disruptive students. Each New Beginning program was supposed to enroll 30 to 60 students. DOE teachers would work inside community-based organizations (CBOs), where CBO staff would provide counseling services while teachers provided academics. Each site was led by an assistant principal. On paper, the concept looked promising, but in practice, it was a cash cow for CBOs and a bust for teachers. Some students benefited from being removed from the traditional setting, but most programs lacked quality teaching and rigorous instruction. Teachers assigned were often new or burned out, and schools sometimes used it as a way to nudge unwanted teachers out.

When I became superintendent, these programs fell under my supervision. I visited each site—we had several in every borough. I remember visiting one in a Bronx housing project. The "school" was located in a basement, with pipes leaking from the ceiling and large rat traps scattered around. I was familiar with mice traps, but these were industrial rat traps. The children were out of control. One student said to me, "Look at where they put us—how do you expect us to act?" It was one of the most profound statements I had ever heard. After visiting, I cried. I couldn't believe children were placed in such conditions. My visit was on a Thursday; by Monday, those students had been relocated to a new site. I didn't ask for permission. I later received a call telling me I wasn't supposed to close sites without authorization. That's when I learned it was better to ask for forgiveness than permission. If I had asked first, nothing would have changed.

I also visited a probation office that had created a makeshift classroom for students. It was appalling. Custodians cleaned only the side of the office where probation officers sat. They ignored the student side—the garbage cans overflowed, and the carpet was never vacuumed.

Later, during a citywide professional development session, a DOE leader claimed she thought the New Beginning program was successful. I publicly disagreed. I'm sure she never forgot my challenge, and probably thought, "Who does he think he is?" But to me, her comments reflected ignorance. I believed that since the children were primarily Black and Brown, she and others like her simply didn't care about the conditions of the program.

If you can control a man's thinking, you do not have to worry about his actions. When you determine what a man shall think, you do not have to concern yourself about what he will do. If you make a man feel that he is inferior, you do not have to compel him to accept an inferior status, for he will seek it himself. If you make a man think that he is justly an outcast, you do not have to order him to the back door. He will go without being told; and if there is no back door, his very nature will demand one.

– Carter Godwin Woodson

No Pass, No Play— Changing the Game On and Off the Court

RELIGION, politics, race, and sports are topics that are sure to result in heated debate or argument. When I became principal at Boys and Girls High School (BGHS), all of these issues seemed to converge through one medium: sports. During my early years at BGHS, the boys' basketball team reached a significant milestone by winning the NYC PSAL Championship at Madison Square Garden. It was a proud moment. However, behind the scenes, there was a looming issue—academic eligibility.

It had become commonplace for teachers to be approached by coaches requesting grade changes or allowances for missed work. This wasn't just a problem at BGHS—it's an ingrained culture in schools across the country. I met with the coaches and issued a stern directive: Do not ask teachers to pass students who are failing. The coach's role was to support athletes academically, not to circumvent standards. I instructed them to hold study halls and enforce accountability.

Many students simply needed structure, while others had been raised in a culture where athletic skills overshadowed academics. That would not be the norm under my leadership. Frequently, prior to a major game, a star athlete's parents—often the mother—would appeal to me, pleading to allow their child to play. To eliminate such conflicts, I implemented a clear academic policy for athletes: complete 30 hours of community service, maintain a 70 average, fail no more than one class, and seniors must pass all classes. Additionally, they had to pass their first-period class, which was often neglected by students across all demographics.

The greatest controversy arose after the boys' basketball team secured their second NYC PSAL Championship. As they prepared to advance to the state championship, half the team was deemed academically ineligible. I upheld the rules and did not allow them to play.

Public pressure mounted from all corners—students, parents, clergy, politicians, media. A sports reporter accused me of using the students to prove a point. I acknowledged the accusation—yes, I was proving a point. Academic achievement must come first. One pastor delivered a sermon on grace, implying I should overlook the students' shortcomings. When he finished, I quietly handed him a few of the students' report cards and asked, "What would Jesus say about this?" That concluded the sermon.

Although the team lost the championship game, I believe we achieved a moral victory. Shortly afterward, a local news station ran a segment titled "No Pass, No Play," which I felt fairly represented the school's stance. A year later, the same reporter who criticized me returned and apologized, saying he finally understood my rationale. I accepted and respected his apology.

The basketball program was a point of pride for the school. They played in national tournaments and had a sponsorship with Under Armour, which supplied the team with athletic apparel, including sneakers. I recall one of the coaches asking my shoe size. I responded, "I don't have a size," but what I meant was, "I don't have a price." Accepting such items would have compromised my integrity.

As our girls' basketball team gained momentum, I noticed Under Armour's lack of support for them compared to the boys' team. When I raised this issue, they responded that the girls didn't carry the same stature. Because they refused to support our girls equitably, I removed their large banner from our gymnasium, and they withdrew their sponsorship. It wasn't a loss—our coach quickly secured a new partnership with Nike.

The boys' basketball coaches loved their players. Though our approaches may have differed, we all wanted the same outcome—success for our students, both on the court and in the classroom.

My No Pass, No Play policy fundamentally changed the sports culture at BGHS. It set a precedent that academics and accountability are non-negotiable. This shift didn't just impact sports—it sent a clear message throughout the school: excellence in the classroom is the first championship every student must win.

PART III

REFLECTIONS FROM THE EDGE

Divine intervention is never a heavenly punishment or transcendental prank. It is a safeguard for our highest good.

—Anthon St. Maarten

Return to the Field

AFTER serving as superintendent of alternative schools for two years, I resigned on July 1, 2005. I was done with the game. I fought the good fight from within the system and believed I could better fight from outside it. So, I started my own educational consulting company. I left behind a job that paid $160,000 a year. In the year following my departure from the NYCDOE, I earned only about $25,000. But I was free—truly free—and freedom, while costly, was worth the slight change in lifestyle.

In addition to consulting, I continued my work with community-based nonprofit organizations—C.L.I.M.B. and R.I.S.E.—both of which were volunteer-based. For reasons I can't fully explain, I always felt richer when I was volunteering.

Almost four years to the day after leaving the NYCDOE, I received an early morning call from Frank Mickens, the former principal of Boys and Girls High School. Our 6:00 a.m. conversations were routine—both of us were early risers—but this morning was different.

I was staying at a Red Roof Inn in Pittsburgh, Pennsylvania, with my friend and colleague, Mark Mainella. We had traveled there to meet with an executive from the Heinz Family Foundation about potential funding for an educational project.

Mickens sounded unlike himself—his usual fire was laced with tension. I pictured him clenching his fists, his long fingernails pressing into his palms. He was concerned that "they" were talking seriously about closing BGHS. Worse still, the principal—his handpicked successor—was about to be removed.

Without thinking, I responded, "If they let me return to the DOE, I'll take the job." I shocked myself. Up until that moment, I hadn't considered returning—especially not as principal of BGHS. That was Mickens' house. But the words were out. He paused, then said, "What! What! Let me get back to you." That's when the wheels of my return began to turn.

Days later, in late June, Mickens called again. He told me that Chancellor Joel Klein agreed to my return as principal of BGHS, where I had once served as an English teacher in the late 1980s. I told Mickens, jokingly, "If I return, you're going to have to handle the fourth floor." He laughed. "Naw, kid." I replied, "No, I'm serious."

After Mickens retired from BGHS, central DOE leadership no longer welcomed him in the building. They pressured his successor to relegate him to the garage in the school's basement. But that garage became his court—he held meetings there with students, staff, and community members who still sought his wisdom. I would bring visitors down there to listen and learn. One of my most touching memories was introducing my daughter to him in that very garage. He had a stuffed Mickey Mouse doll she loved. Mickens, despite his rough exterior, had a heart that children instinctively trusted.

I was scheduled to officially begin as principal of BGHS in July. I imagined Mickens, regal and unbothered, sitting in his big leather chair in the middle of the fourth-floor corridor. Some principals may have felt intimidated stepping into a role that Mickens had defined. I wasn't. I knew I wouldn't be filling his shoes—I was standing on his shoulders.

On the morning of July 8, 2009, I sat in my SUV outside Teachers College at Columbia University, waiting for the meter to start so I could attend class. I was a doctoral student in the Urban Education Leadership program. Mickens and I had our usual morning call. That morning, he talked about Michael Jackson, James Brown, and Reverend Al Sharpton. He noted that Sharpton had delivered the eulogies for both Jackson and Brown. "Al Sharpton is no joke!" he exclaimed. I told him I had to go—my class was starting, and it was time to feed the meter. We agreed to talk the next morning.

For some reason, I didn't call him the next morning. I was back at Teachers College when I received a phone call from David Banks.

"Have you heard about Mickens?" he asked.

"No," I replied.

"He passed this morning."

I don't remember much after that.

A member of his family later asked me to speak at his funeral. I spoke about how some of those present had once turned their backs on him. I also reflected on our last conversation—the one about Reverend Sharpton. In a beautiful twist of fate, Reverend Al Sharpton gave the eulogy at Mickens' funeral. It was profound.

Shortly after Mickens' passing, I officially became the principal of Boys and Girls High School. I remember speaking to him in spirit and saying, "Yo, you were supposed to get the fourth floor!"

Speak with any urban school leader, and they will tell you that one of their greatest challenges is managing ineffective and resistant staff.

—Bernard Gassaway

Courage to Confront Incompetence

I remember during the beginning of my second year as principal of Boys and Girls High School, I held an orientation for incoming students. We shared routine information about our programs and bell schedules via a PowerPoint presentation projected on a large screen in the auditorium. During my remarks to the parents, I made a statement that would ripple through the school community: I told them that the hardest part of my job was deciding which students would get the bad teachers.

That statement never sat well with staff, but the parents received it as an uncomfortable truth about the public school system. I may have been the first public school official they had encountered who told them that truth so plainly.

By that time, I had played the game long enough. I knew, based on experience, that underperforming teachers often found permanent homes in public schools—especially in those that served predominantly Black and low-income communities. This was not just anecdotal; national statistics consistently support the claim.

Because it was extremely difficult to remove ineffective teachers, many school leaders resorted to what became known as "passing the lemons." This practice involved encouraging incompetent teachers to transfer to another school, where they would continue to do harm. These teachers remained in the system because of a strong union that negotiated protections, including a no-layoff policy.

Let me clarify what I mean when I say a teacher was incompetent. I am referring to those who made the conscious decision not to plan or prepare for lessons. In some cases, even when they did plan, they failed to deliver instruction effectively. Incompetence was not confined to the classroom; I witnessed it at every level—assistant principals, principals, and even assistant superintendents. I made it my duty to remove anyone who was not doing their job, especially those tasked with supervising and supporting teachers.

I recall a meeting in my conference room with the United Federation of Teachers President Michael Mulgrew and retired Vice President Sterling Roberson. Roberson requested that I stop using percentages or specific numbers when speaking to the press. The meeting was prompted by concern from my highly influential advisory council—comprised of political, state, and community leaders—who provided me with the political cover that allowed me to survive in my role as long as I did. Without that support, it would have been nearly impossible to be so candid and vocal about the failures of the system that employed me.

But I was unafraid of losing my job, so I operated without fear. I felt an obligation to speak honestly to parents. I made it clear that I was not satisfied with the quality of instruction their children were receiving. But saying it wasn't enough—I had a responsibility to do something about it.

I approached teacher development with energy and commitment. I identified four categories of teachers:

1. Willing and able
2. Willing but unable
3. Unwilling but able
4. Unwilling and unable

The last group posed the greatest threat. I could offer them the best professional development and unlimited support, but it would amount to nothing if they weren't interested in improving. And still, these individuals stood in front of children every day. I never apologized for my stance against these teachers and administrators. My goal was to remove them from the profession.

That was easier said than done. It took years. One year, I managed to initiate five 3020-a hearings—the disciplinary process for tenured educators in New York. While most principals struggle to get one such case filed, I made it a priority. Yet, even five successful filings felt like a drop in the bucket.

Still, I must acknowledge the other half of my staff—the 50% who were willing and able to serve students with excellence. They were champions for children and stalwarts of the profession. Many privately supported my mission to remove ineffective teachers, even if they maintained a united front in public.

As a superintendent, I didn't stop. I removed assistant superintendents, district administrators, and principals who failed to perform. These decisions were rarely difficult. The evidence was clear, and clarity made action easier. Unlike tenured teachers, many of these administrators lacked union protections and served at the discretion of the Chancellor.

Speak with any urban school leader, and they will tell you that one of their greatest challenges is managing ineffective and resistant staff. I do not regret my efforts—fruitless though they sometimes were—to confront incompetence head-on. And I certainly do not regret telling parents the truth. Too often, school and district officials view parents as problems rather than partners. I chose the opposite. I saw truth as the bridge.

No significant learning can occur without a significant relationship.

—James Comer

Rituals That Built Trust

WHEN I served as principal at Beach Channel High School and later at Boys and Girls High School, I adopted two daily rituals that anchored my leadership: greeting students every morning and being present outside during dismissal. These moments were sacred to me—especially the mornings—and nothing short of an emergency interrupted them. That time was for the students.

Each day, I would say "Good morning" or "What's up" to every student I encountered. This was more than a routine greeting; it was a vital part of my work. These few minutes allowed me to gauge the emotional temperature of the day. I developed an instinct for reading body language and could often sense what kind of day lay ahead—especially for students navigating hostile environments before arriving at school. Their body language told me everything: stern faces, tense posture, and guarded steps often revealed that their walk to school had been a battle.

There were mornings when I intercepted potential altercations before they began. I could detect aggression in a student's silence or the way they carried themselves. I'd step in personally or discreetly signal a dean or school safety agent to monitor the situation. Just as often, I'd notice a student who looked especially burdened. Without making a scene, I'd ask a social worker or support staff member to check in with them.

I'll never forget one particular morning. A student walked into the building with a demeanor that pierced my heart. I quietly asked someone to escort her to the school social worker. Moments later, I went to check in. I found the social worker walking the girl down the first-floor corridor. She told me, "The student found her mother dead this morning." Shocked, I asked where she was taking her. The social worker replied, "I called a cab to send her home."

I was floored. Why would anyone send a grieving student back to an empty home? I later learned that the only reason the student came to school was to be with her favorite teacher. I quickly arranged for staff to cover that teacher's class so the student could get the support she truly needed. That incident stayed with me. I could not envision someone with so little empathy remaining in our school. I removed that social worker from the building by the end of the year.

Everyone on staff understood that my morning ritual was not to be interrupted. BGHS officially opened its doors at 7:30 a.m. If the doors didn't open exactly on time, a particular group of students would bang to be let in. There were about eight of them—students with special needs who functioned on strict routines. They gathered every morning to claim their corner of the cafeteria, which served as their safe haven. Making sure the doors opened on time was part of my silent contract with them.

My dismissal ritual was just as critical. I stood outside with deans and school safety agents to ensure students felt safe leaving school. I remember one afternoon when I went out a bit earlier than usual. I stood on the corner of Fulton and Utica—an area the students called "the circle." This was a known hotspot for conflict. On that day, an eerie calmness filled the air. Like an owl, I scanned in every direction, alert.

Suddenly, about 50 young people came charging toward where I was standing. I barely had time to step aside before they rushed past me, heading into the subway station. A massive brawl erupted—thankfully, before our students were dismissed. I was shaken but undeterred. The next day, I resumed my place at the circle. Nothing was going to make me abandon my post.

These rituals were not my invention. I learned them from my mentor and friend, Frank Mickens. I watched him do this every single day, and I carried that wisdom into my own practice.

Nearly 20 years after my tenure at Beach Channel, I stood at Penn Station waiting for my train. A young White man approached me. "Are you Mr. Gassaway?" he asked. I said yes. "You may not remember me," he continued, "but I was one of your students at Beach Channel. I just want to thank you. Every morning, you were outside saying good morning to us. That made us feel safe."

He was right—I didn't remember him. But I remembered the ritual, and now I was witnessing the power of delayed gratification. That moment validated everything.

Whoever controls the media controls the mind.

—Jim Morrison

Media Relations

FROM the onset of my leadership, particularly at Beach Channel High School, I enjoyed a relatively positive relationship with the press. When I first arrived at BCHS, I was introduced to The WAVE, a popular community newspaper that has long been a staple in the Far Rockaway and Belle Harbor communities. I appreciated their honest and fair reporting, which reflected the kind of balanced journalism the media should practice. I read the paper weekly to keep up with community news, and as the school's image began to improve, writers at The WAVE acknowledged the turnaround. One article, published on January 15, 2000, titled "Beach Channel's Comeback," stated: "It took leadership. It took vision. It took courage. These ingredients were combined to return Beach Channel High School to its heyday, a school Rockawayites could be proud of. Leading this charge, with a group of dedicated and determined teachers, was Bernard Gassaway, the principal of Beach Channel."

I recall asking The WAVE if a student could contribute a weekly article about school events. This strategy would give students a platform to write while also generating positive press for the school. Beach Channel also had its own in-house publication, SeaScope, which was widely distributed within the school. I do not recall any major challenges with our school paper.

My relationship with The WAVE shifted during one encounter with a reporter who asked to meet me. Though unsure of his reasons, I agreed. We met outside the school, and he handed me an anonymous letter sent to him. He told me he did not intend to publish it, recognizing my efforts and perhaps rewarding them through his discretion. That act solidified my trust in the integrity of The WAVE's staff and editors, and it strengthened my confidence in dealing with the press moving forward.

One of my guiding principles was to make myself accessible to the press. I expected honesty in their reporting. We did not need to agree on the final story, but honesty was non-negotiable.

At Boys and Girls High School, I had a notable interaction with Yoav Gonen, a reporter from *The New York Post*. Gonen had a reputation for being critical of public schools. Before agreeing to his visit, I consulted with Marge Fienberg from the NYCDOE Press Office, who asked if I was sure I wanted him inside the school. I told her I had no problem walking the halls with any reporter, so she approved. I only gave Gonen one condition: he could report only on what he observed. He agreed. On the day of his visit, despite an injured foot that required him to wear a brace, he toured the building with me. Normally, I avoided elevators to stay visible to students and staff, but I took it that day for his sake. As students transitioned between periods, Gonen asked, 'Is it always like this?'—referring to the calm and positive atmosphere. I answered honestly: "No. Some days there are fights, and when that happens, we break them up and move on." I do not recall him ever publishing an article about that visit, or even during my tenure afterward, but he occasionally reached out with inquiries. My rule remained clear: I only spoke on the record. I avoided speaking off the record because I considered it cowardly. If something needed to be said, I would say it openly. I believed members of the press respected my candor.

A similar approach guided my interaction with Leslie Brody, a reporter who later published an article in *The Wall Street Journal* on September 26, 2014, titled "Brooklyn's Boys and Girls High School Fights Failure: Critics Say City Hasn't Done Enough to Help Troubled Students; Plan Is Overdue." I insisted she could only report what she observed or what my students shared. While I understood that every reporter came with an angle, I emphasized fairness because I was granting her direct access to my students. Overall, I considered her reporting fair, even though I was well aware of *The Wall Street Journal's* preference for charter schools as a cost-effective model.

Coverage of Boys and Girls High School, in general, was relatively fair, especially considering the Department of Education's often guarded posture toward the press. I understood their caution—schools inevitably experience moments that are not favorable. Still, I believed the role of the press was to report truthfully, though fairness was often more aspiration than reality.

Through my experiences, I learned that strong relationships with reporters and editors must be built on respect and trust. I also came to understand the varying influence of different media outlets. Local community publications differ from citywide newspapers, which differ from state or national publications. At the international level, outlets like *The New York Times* carried enormous weight. On October 10, 2014, they published "Principal of Failing Brooklyn School Quits, Saying City Lacks an Education Plan." I also had a positive relationship with the *New York Amsterdam News*, which I consider to be both local and national in reach.

Our Time Press, a Brooklyn-based publication, also provided fair and honest reporting. However, I once learned a difficult lesson after a phone interview with their editor. When the article was published, I was horrified to see my casual speech—including every "um"—printed verbatim. Initially, I blamed the editor, but I eventually realized the responsibility was mine. I had been too comfortable, forgetting that everything said on record might be published.

Another lesson came from a television interview with ABC News. I was interviewed for over an hour about the decision to close GED sites across the city. The final segment that aired was less than two minutes long, edited in a way that distorted the context. Frustrated, I resolved only to appear in live interviews going forward. This led to more candid exchanges with programs like Errol Louis's Inside City Hall and Good Day New York on Fox 5. Live interviews left less room for narratives to be reshaped.

Eventually, I realized the greatest empowerment came from writing my own narratives. I began submitting articles and letters to outlets such as *The New York Times*, *Albany Times Union*, *Queens Chronicle*, *New York Amsterdam News*, and *Education Week*. By telling my own story, I ensured it would not be reframed by someone else.

Before consenting to interviews, I always researched a reporter's prior work to understand their style. I did not seek advantage or agreement, only fairness and honesty. These principles guided every interaction I had with the press.

Unbought and unbossed.

—Shirley Chisholm

WHAT IS YOUR PRICE

DURING my early tenure as a school leader, I witnessed district leaders place toxic, harmful, and incompetent staff in school buildings to work directly with children, usually the most vulnerable. I wondered if their decisions were made easier because they were distanced from children.

I began many of my educational leadership courses with this question: "What is your price?" Many aspiring school leaders look puzzled or confused by the question. After a momentary pause, I added, "How much would it cost for you to look the other way when children are being hurt under your watch?" Often, they react by shaking their heads, indicating that they do not have a price. I remind them about the car note, mortgage, college loans, and a host of other financial obligations that they have. "How will you pay your bills if you do not have a job?" This is when things get interesting. People begin to pause to really consider the question: "What is my price?" It depends on the situation.

One of the first things I was told when I arrived at Beach Channel High School (BCHS) as principal in April 1997 was, "We handle things in-house." I did not understand the gravity of this edict until I witnessed a very influential union-connected teacher have a

16–17-year-old female student sitting on his lap in his classroom. I followed the obligatory reporting protocol (Office of Special Investigations). At that time, you could request that the accused could be removed pending the outcome of the investigation.

About two months after the allegation was reported and the teacher's removal, one day while standing in the first-floor corridor, I heard what sounded like adults cheering and clapping. As I arrived at the main entrance, I saw several staff members greeting, clapping and welcoming the teacher back. I had not received word that he would be returned. In fact, I was not informed about the findings of the investigation. He was removed as scum of the earth, and returned as a hero—Mr. Untouchable. Unbeknown to me, he was probably one of hundreds who were returned to their schools that year, if they were even removed. This was a very powerful message to me about the "system's" care and concern for children. Understand that the "system" is a collection of adults who place little value on the health and well-being of children.

When the "system" returned this teacher to the building, they unleashed a torrent of toxicity. This was also a time when anonymous allegations against me increased. I learned that there was one definite price you would pay as a leader who sought to protect children.

I remember another situation when I was principal at BCHS during my fifth year. A teacher was accused of hitting a student. I reported the incident and requested that the teacher be removed pending the outcome of the investigation. One or two months later, I met with the superintendent of Queens high schools and a New York City Board of Education lawyer. We met so that they could tell me about the outcome of the investigation. Upon reflection, it was not customary to have a meeting regarding the outcome of an investigation. They informed me that the claim of corporal punishment had been substantiated. I thought great. Then they informed me that the teacher would be returning to the school. I told them, "He cannot come back!" The lawyer was empathetic that he would return. When the superintendent interjected, to align with the lawyer, I stressed that he would not return to the school. The lawyer said I had dropped the ball. I did not understand what she meant. I again said, "He cannot come back." She asked me, "Who do you think you are?" I said, "The principal." I said it as it had a ring of authority. I followed by saying, "If he returns to Beach Channel, I will resign on the spot!" This statement was not premeditated. It was like an out-of-body experience. As I drove back to the school, I thought, How am I going to explain this to my wife. How would this play out when I return to the school?

After speaking with my assistant principal of security (my confidant), he began to rally the students to protest on my behalf. I quickly stopped this pending protest. I never wanted to put children at the center of any of my battles. I was the one to fight their battles, not the other way around.

Within a day or two, I was notified that the teacher would not be returned to Beach Channel. Experiences like this reminded me that I had no price. No job or amount of money could persuade me to turn my back on children and pretend that they are not being hurt. This accounts for my public advocacy on their behalf.

While I understand the politics of education, I do not understand how easy it is for some people to look the other way, mainly to avoid jeopardizing their job security.

What is it about the system that makes educators have to choose between protecting children or protecting the system? If the system is truly designed to educate, nurture, and protect children, there would never be the need for such a choice.

Once I did not fear losing my job, I was free to advocate on behalf of children without hesitation.

You don't make progress by standing on the sidelines, whimpering and complaining. You make progress by implementing ideas. If they don't give you a seat at the table, bring a folding chair.

—Shirley Chisholm

LEADING BLACK

LEADING Black is about protecting children of all races and creeds. My greatest disappointment and bewilderment came from not understanding how some Black educators could overtly and covertly harm children under their care—especially children who looked like them and shared similar experiences. While I believe wholeheartedly that Black educators play a significant role in Black children's lives, that does not mean all Black educators are good for Black children. I have always emphasized that the most important color of a teacher is not skin, but care.

A question posed by a current educational leader once triggered a flurry of memories for me: "Why do I always have to fight?" She was referring to her constant bureaucratic battles—fights that often arise when one is determined to improve services and conditions for poor and Black children.

I often felt conflicted working within the New York City public education system. I believed the system never truly put children first—despite the slogan used during the Bloomberg administration. In reality, they certainly did not put Black and poor children first. Race is an inescapable reality in public education.

I cannot recall a time when I did not face resistance

because of my race. As a Black leader, I knew that people within and outside of the system would see my race before knowing anything else about me. They would also see the race of my students, arriving with a set of assumptions—often negative.

When I was principal of Beach Channel High School, we began what became an exemplary partnership with Southampton College. I remember taking my staff, mostly White, on a professional development trip to the college, whose faculty was also majority White. During the visit, I overheard one of my White teachers say to a faculty member, "Gassaway is good for the kids, but not for the teachers." I confronted him indirectly during a later faculty meeting, but I never asked him directly what he meant. I cannot imagine he would have made that same comment had I been White.

During the Bloomberg administration, there was a push to close Boys and Girls High School. At that time, I was the only person standing between the school remaining open or being closed and repurposed. When the deputy chancellor proposed renaming or restructuring the school, I told him I would respond after consulting with my community. His reply was, "Who gives a fuck about the community?" On one hand, I appreciated his honesty—his words reflected the true sentiments of the administration and the mayor. On the other hand, his words made it clear that my community, largely Black, did not matter. And if they did not matter, neither did I, as a child of that community.

Frank Mickens, the former principal of BGHS, had posters around the school. One stands out in my memory: "Whose Kids? Our Kids." I fully adopted this belief from the moment I became a teacher and carried it throughout my leadership. Fighting for your own children is different from fighting for strangers. It is personal. If you cannot see yourself in your students, you should leave—because staying is a disservice. When Mickens yelled, "Nobody messes with my kids!" he meant it, and I embraced that belief wholeheartedly.

I led every battle with the conviction that my children deserved the very best. I wanted their experiences to mirror those of children in wealthier communities.

In July 2003, I became superintendent of the alternative schools and programs of the New York City public schools during the Bloomberg administration. It was the second year of mayoral control, with Joel Klein serving as chancellor. I would not have been chosen for the role if not for Dr. Lester Young, Jr., who was serving as executive director. Anyone familiar with education knew Dr. Young was more qualified than Klein to serve as chancellor. Still, Bloomberg chose Klein, who was wise enough to hire Dr. Young to play a vital role in his administration. I credit Dr. Young for any success I achieved as superintendent.

During my first year as superintendent, I applied to become a Revson Fellow at Columbia University. This fellowship brought together a distinguished cohort of community leaders, including Elombe Brath and Esperanza Martell. I was elated to learn of my acceptance, but that joy was quickly tempered when Michele Cahill, a senior member of Klein's administration, told me I would not be able to accept. I later learned she knew of my acceptance because she was a Revson alum. Within 30 minutes of receiving her directive, I informed Dr. Young, who assured me I could accept. Cahill's attempt to block my blessing was thwarted by Dr. Young—an example of power, specifically Black power. I raise race here because I cannot imagine a White superintendent being denied such an opportunity. There is ample evidence to support that assertion.

My tenure as superintendent was relatively short— just two years. During my second year, Dr. Young left the NYCDOE. Shortly after, I was summoned to a meeting with Michael Best, a NYCDOE lawyer, and Klein's chief of staff at Tweed headquarters. They informed me that while Chancellor Klein would be my supervisor on paper, Cahill would be my actual supervisor. She lacked the state certification to be my supervisor of record—meaning she was not even qualified for the role. It was a valuable lesson: job qualifications only matter when those in power want them to matter.

Following that meeting, I had a bad feeling. For some reason, I thought of Emmett Till. I did not believe things would go well with Cahill. She later came to my office in Jamaica, Queens, and instructed me to meet her at

Tweed every Monday morning for debriefings and weekly planning. I suggested instead that we meet at one of our alternative schools. She refused. I said no. I would not allow myself to be controlled, which is what her demand represented. Not long after, in 2005, I resigned from my position as superintendent.

Interestingly, during my tenure, I was never invited to attend the monthly superintendents' meetings. Was it because I was a Black man? The problem with leading while Black is that you never really know. You only know how it feels.

PART IV

PUBLISHED WORKS

BLACK LEADERSHIP EQUALS HOPE FOR EDUCATIONAL TRANSFORMATION

BY DR. BERNARD GASSAWAY, ORIGINALLY PUBLISHED IN OUR TIME PRESS, MAY 27, 2021

WE are in a unique position in the history of the State of New York. For the first time, African Americans hold two out of three of the most powerful leadership positions in state government. The speaker of the New York State Assembly is Carl E. Heastie from the Bronx. He is the first Black person to hold this position. The majority leader of the New York State Senate is Andrea Stewart-Cousins from Westchester County. She is the first woman to hold this position.

Arguably, other than the governor, these are the two most powerful government officials in New York.

Their power rests largely in their ability to set the state's agendas, which includes establishing budget priorities, state policies and laws.

I will highlight their roles and influence in setting the state's education agenda.

According to Article XI of the New York State Constitution, "The legislature shall provide for the maintenance and support of a system of free common schools, wherein all the children of this state may be educated." This means the legislators, not the governor, are responsible for education in the State of New York.

The legislature specifically maintains and supports education through the appointment of the members of the New York State Board of Regents. Currently, there are 17 members. Each of the state's 13 judicial districts has one representative, and four regents serve as at-large representatives. All 17 members are appointed by the legislature to serve unpaid five-year terms.

Before the appointment of the current chancellor of the New York State Board of Regents, Dr. Lester Young, Jr., Vice-Chancellor Emerita Dr. Adelaide Sanford was the highest-ranking woman of African ancestry on the Board of Regents until her departure in 2007.

Although the New York State Board of Regents wields a tremendous amount of authority, it works in relative anonymity. In speaking with hundreds of educators and community stakeholders, few have any knowledge of the regents' role.

The Regents serve as a board of education for the state. According to their website, the Regents "are responsible for the general supervision of all educational activities within the State, presiding over The University and the New York State Education Department." In addition to a host of other responsibilities, they hire the state's commissioner of education.

Interestingly, probably for the first time in the history of the New York State Board of Regents, most of its members are people of color. What does this mean for the quality of education for children of African ancestry, who have been largely disenfranchised by public school systems across New York?

For many years, Vice Chancellor Emerita Dr. Sanford was a lone voice on the Board of Regents. She fought fearlessly for all children, but for children of African ancestry in particular. Many of the current members of the Board are there largely because of her legacy.

Under the current leadership of Chancellor Young and New York State Education Commissioner Dr. Betty A. Rosa, the Board of Regents is embarking on an ambitious diversity, equity, and inclusion agenda. Because these concepts evoke fear in some people, the Board of Regents has only touched on them tangentially.

Because conservative forces will surely organize against any effort to address the lack of diversity, equity, and inclusion in public schools comprehensively, it is important that people who recognize the importance of such policies stand up and speak out.

I have witnessed White communities organize and demand action from their leaders, particularly on educational matters, with success. We (people of the African diaspora, Asian, Latinx, Indigenous and poor people, as well as people with disabilities) need to do the same. Let us be reminded of the profound wisdom of Dr. Martin Luther King, Jr., who said, "The time is always right to do what is right."

If you believe in a public education system grounded in diversity, equity, and inclusion, let your state and local officials hear your voice. Your silence signals submission to and acceptance of the status quo.

THE PUBLIC SCHOOL SYSTEM IS RIGGED AGAINST POOR AND BLACK CHILDREN

BY DR. BERNARD GASSAWAY,
ORIGINALLY PUBLISHED IN HUFFPOST, MAY 6, 2017

THE American public school system is failing. Not because of children. Not because of poverty. But because the game is rigged.

After working nearly 30 years as an urban school educator, I am convinced beyond a reasonable doubt that the rules of the public school game are rigged against poor and Black children. The guardians of the game focus on three strategies to rig it: deception, fear, and misinformation.

As a former public school insider, I see and understand how politicians and educators deceive the public, manipulating data to draw pictures of progress, which in many instances are nothing more than illusions. An increase in high school graduation rates does not mean the students are ready for college or careers. An increase in college enrollment does not mean a higher college completion rate. A decrease in student suspension rates does not mean the school environment is safer. Achieving a level of proficiency on standardized tests does not mean one can think and grasp complex concepts.

"The emphasis on standardized tests may be the most damaging type of deception that public schools practice."

The emphasis on standardized tests may be the most damaging type of deception that public schools practice. Politicians persistently pressure public school personnel to produce improved standardized test results, which are the main measurement of school quality. This places teachers in a dilemma. They either teach to the test, as often directed by school administrators, or they risk their job security.

Arguably, many people become teachers because they love teaching. Most probably had no idea to what extent politics would influence their teaching practice. They quickly learn that standardized testing is the most politically charged aspect of their job. Ironically, teachers are not taught to teach to the test. Yet, this practice of teaching to the test dominates their pedagogy on all levels, particularly grades 3 through 12. Furthermore, the overemphasis on test prep robs children of quality instructional time, not to mention limiting any attempts at creativity by teachers.

Teachers know that if their students' tests scores are low, they face the threat of a negative rating or termination. This is one reason they support unions: job security.

Other than collective bargaining, the job of teachers' unions is basically twofold: increase and retain membership. The more members there are, the more money unions raise by collecting dues, money that can be used to lobby politicians for more and stronger job protections as well as higher salaries. In this scenario, children only matter because each child comes with a dollar amount. That is one reason unions fight against any form of school choice. Parents who pull their children out of public school hurt the unions' bottom line: money.

Of all stakeholders in public education, parents are the least informed. After all, the public school game can only be played if parents put their children in the game. However, the recent rise in the number of public charter schools is causing parents to explore other options for their children. This is a game changer.

Charter school operators successfully market their schools as the better option. They use standardized test scores to make their point. However, the truth is, when it comes to student outcomes, there is very little difference between traditional public schools and public charter schools. Because of superior marketing and student recruitment strategies, charter operators have convinced a substantial number of parents that their schools are the better option.

There is evidence to support the claim that some charter school leaders pressure children with special needs to attend their local public schools. It is also true that some low-performing children are encouraged to leave charter schools. It is, however, ironic that public school educators speak out against this practice when they are guilty of doing the same. It is harder to detect the push-out strategy in traditional public schools because of their size, particularly in New York City, whose public school system serves slightly over 1 million children.

As a former public school student, teacher, assistant principal, principal, and superintendent, I know firsthand the potential of a public school education. Public school educators, by and large, are some of the most dedicated, compassionate, competent, and caring people I have worked with.

Unfortunately, in public schools that serve majority of poor and Black children, teachers, parents, and children are used as pawns to perpetuate a system that remains unchanged because of deception, fear, and misinformation.

PUBLIC SCHOOL OFFICIALS ARE ARTIFICIALLY INFLATING GRADUATION RATES. I'VE SEEN IT MYSELF

BY DR. BERNARD GASSAWAY, ORIGINALLY PUBLISHED IN EDWEEK, AUGUST 29, 2017

AS a direct result of a public thirst for schools to show progress, boards of education pressure superintendents, superintendents squeeze principals, principals ride teachers, and teachers stress students. The ultimate measure of progress for schools nationwide is high school graduation rates.

Public school officials use a variety of schemes to give the appearance of progress.

Credit recovery is one strategy that school officials use to allow students to quickly make up for classes they have failed, without receiving formal instruction. Credit recovery is a national practice, though it may be called

something else. In fact, "credit recovery" is a broad term
that encompasses multiple strategies, some more effective
than others. Blended learning, virtual learning, after-
school programs, summer school, weekend school, and
night school are all credit-recovery strategies.

I experienced the worst of this practice when I
became principal of New York City's Boys and Girls High
School in 2009. One student was told by his teacher to
complete about five handouts to make up for a summer
school art course. Instead of attending class, that student
was allowed to participate in a basketball tournament in
Las Vegas. (I denied the student credit and eliminated this
abusive practice.)

Also, students with disabilities often have a lower
threshold for meeting graduation requirements. Some
school officials resort to reclassifying struggling students
to increase their graduation rates. By reclassifying general
education students, they become eligible for a lower
graduation threshold. In the case of New York state,
students with individualized education plans are currently
required to pass a single English- and a single math-exit
exam to meet graduation requirements, rather than the
five such exams that are required for general education
students.

Public school officials use a variety of schemes to give
the appearance of progress.

In my experience, school officials entice parents
to become complicit, as officials encourage them to

request for their children a plan under Section 504 of the Rehabilitation Act of 1973, which includes a more expansive definition of disability than is protected under the Individuals with Disabilities Education Act. That 504 plan allows certain general education students to receive some of the same accommodations that students with IEPs receive: extended time; having the exam read to them; and, in select cases, even a lower score threshold to pass exit exams.

Lastly, when education officials cannot use any of the aforementioned tactics to get struggling students through high school, they transfer or push out students who are off-track for graduation—dropping the dead weight that is dragging down graduation statistics. Pushing students out is the most efficient way to increase a school's graduation rate. Principals transfer overage and undercredited students to alternative schools.

That, too, is an abusive practice I've observed firsthand. Here's how it works: Principals and guidance counselors tell students they must leave the school if they want to graduate. Students are persuaded to transfer to alternative schools under the guise that it is easier for them to earn credits and graduate. In some cases, those same school personnel even inform students that they are not allowed to return, thus rendering these schools no longer accountable for the students' performance indicators.

In New York, state education officials reported an increase in the 2015 high school graduation rate to 78 percent, a slight rise from the previous years. In 2016, that number increased to 79.4 percent, coinciding with the introduction of the New York state regents' new graduation requirements. The state's standardized high school exam offers new graduation standards for students with disabilities by reducing the number of exit examinations from five to two. Once standards have been lowered and the rigor associated with the new requirements lessened, these seemingly better graduation numbers are no longer valid measures of students' achievement.

It is time for state education officials to act morally and provide specific guidance to local school districts to stop these known abusive and fraudulent practices, which ultimately harm the very children whom schools are supposed to serve.

Schools & Race Relations: A Toxic Topic, by Dr. Bernard Gassaway, originally published in Gassaway Word Blog, November 1, 2016

As an educator, I am deeply disturbed by fellow educators' apparent fear to engage in meaningful discussions about race relations with each other and with children.

As many teachers have shared with me, discussing race relations can be challenging, if not downright frightening. Some fear that their subconscious biases and prejudices might surface during a conversation, and they might say something offensive. Others fear losing their jobs if they say the "wrong" thing.

Teachers have expressed that they welcome meaningful professional development regarding race relations. Unfortunately, school leaders do not appear to know how or where to begin because, in fact, they share the same fears that many teachers have.

SCHOOLS & RACE RELATIONS: A TOXIC TOPIC

BY DR. BERNARD GASSAWAY,
ORIGINALLY PUBLISHED IN
GASSAWAY WORD BLOG,
NOVEMBER 1, 2016

AS an educator, I am deeply disturbed by fellow educators' apparent fear to engage in meaningful discussions about race relations with each other and with children

As many teachers have shared with me, discussing race relations can be challenging, if not downright frightening. Some fear that their subconscious biases and prejudices might surface during a conversation, and they might say something offensive. Others fear losing their jobs if they say the "wrong" thing.

Teachers have expressed that they welcome meaningful professional development regarding race relations. Unfortunately, school leaders do not appear to know how or where to begin because, in fact, they share the same fears that many teachers have.

Race Relations Challenges in School Communities

Discussions on race relations are practically absent from school professional development activities. While teachers admit that race relations are extremely important, school and district leaders put minimal resources towards addressing this important topic.

One challenge for educational leaders is that they do not know how to begin to address race relations. They are not aware of organizations that specialize in leading race-based discussions and strategies in the workplace.

Race discussions can be toxic if they are not organized around specific objectives. Simply talking about race issues is not enough. In fact, talk without action can actually exacerbate the problem.

Some school districts find it difficult to engage in meaningful discussions about race because they lack a critical mass of people of color to contribute to the dialogue.

Other school districts avoid race discussions until a racially charged incident occurs in their school community. Once the dust settles, they go back to business as usual.

Effects of Inaction

Some public school personnel (teachers and principals) have long sat on the sidelines during numerous racial crises. Their inaction only contributes to larger societal challenges. Here are some truisms:

Communities segregate. Schools segregate. Teachers segregate. Students segregate.

Nothing is done to establish sustainable practices for dealing with the root causes of racism, which are admittedly beyond the control of school systems.

To avoid race discussions in schools is to contribute to the seeding of segregation.

Segregation breeds contempt, distrust and fear.

Strategies to Address Race Relations in Schools

Engage in action-oriented race-based discussions. They are meaningless if they stop post-talk. To be meaningful, these discussions require continuous and strategic engagement.

Strive for organic engagement. Organic engagement occurs when people who share similar interests or causes gather to plan, discuss and act on what they believe.

Be strategic. Strategic engagement involves consistently meeting and working to prevent problems that might occur, rather than merely responding to race-based problems as they arise.

Invite and engage community stakeholders in meaningful ways. By inviting stakeholders to participate in the learning environment, you allow them to contribute to learning experiences for children and staff. Stakeholders can infuse life into a lifeless curriculum.

Work with the community (seek diversity) to infuse culture into the school environment. The ultimate goal is for the school to truly become part of the community, rather than an institution located with a community.

Be intentional about diversity in your hiring. It is not enough to talk about diversity. It must be practiced.

Conclusion

The responsibility for improving race relations does not rest solely on the shoulders of one people, entity or race. Rather, each individual or organization bears the responsibility for addressing this problem.

However, I believe that, as educators, we have a greater responsibility and opportunity to confront and combat racism, beginning in the workplace. Our value to society is diminished when we do not address the reality that our children and we face.

While community and neighborhood segregation are harmful to race relations, segregated schools are catastrophic. We can change this swiftly, though courage is required on the part of the school, the district, and the political leadership.

Unless we change policies and practices (particularly

in public schools), to paraphrase the prophetic pronouncement of the former Governor of Alabama George Wallace, we will continue to suffer from "racism today, racism tomorrow, and racism forever."

Our silence about racism does not make it go away.

Hempstead Community: Black Public School Children Don't Matter

Dr. Bernard Gassaway,

originally published in HuffPost, July 13, 2017

LET'S agree that Black children in Hempstead don't matter. Then we can stop the charade and the futile efforts to change and improve schools under the guise of caring about children.

I find it extremely troubling that too many people have accepted, through their actions, that Black children do not matter. I am not one of them.

The purpose of this message is to focus on ways residents of Hempstead can change from accepting an education culture of dysfunction, corruption, and incompetence to promoting and supporting a culture of community, care, and competence. This can best be demonstrated by strategically and conscientiously investing in our children's education.

A responsive and accountable school governance structure is essential to a good educational system. Hempstead's current public-school governance (its school board) is dysfunctional and corrupt, which makes it impossible for children in Hempstead to receive a quality education. What is required to change the school board's unaccountable, nonresponsive, and irreverent culture? First, let's explore how we got here. Then we can focus on how to change.

People remember where they were when President John F. Kennedy was assassinated. They remember when Dr. Martin Luther King, Jr. was murdered by an assassin's bullet.

As longtime Hempstead residents, where were you when the hope of public school children of Hempstead was assassinated? When did the despicable and deplorable acts of corruption begin? Why does this continual cycle of corruption and incompetence persist, with apparent acceptance from community stakeholders, including politicians, clergy, residents, parents, teachers, and school officials?

By any reasonable measure, the Hempstead Public School Board is depressingly dysfunctional. Sadly, this reality is likely to continue unless the community residents awake from the deep and depressing disposition of believing and accepting that things won't change.

Too many people in Hempstead appear to accept the current school system and are convinced that things will never change because that's the way it has been, that's the way it is, and that's way it will always be.

When I speak to residents of Hempstead about public schools, they speak of the school system with such dispassion and disconnection. Educators whisper for fear of retribution, especially if they live in Hempstead. Some quietly argue that too many people who work in the system got their jobs through corruption—this reminds me of the Machiavellian notion of the ends justifying the means.

Here's what I know. We cannot blame children. Among all stakeholders, children are the most resilient. They are geniuses and deserve a fertile foundation from which to learn and excel.

We cannot blame parents because they have limited to no options other than what the public school system has to offer, which is not much considering the overcrowding conditions and outdated infrastructure of school facilities, not to mention the poor quality of instruction and the limited course offerings.

I will not accept that Hempstead is hopeless, as many longtime residents seem to believe.

I offer the following immediate steps to begin to address the dysfunctional, corrupt, and incompetent school board. However, you should know that any effort

to improve the public school system must be based on
common individual and community beliefs and values.

We must:

- Invest in our children. Address the education crisis as if it were a life-threatening virus.
  Repurpose our current spending patterns to
  maximize available funding.
- Value family. Organize weekly and monthly
  activities to bring families together.
- Value community. Organize weekly and monthly
  activities to bring residents together.
- Organize local clergy to strategize on how to
  support and empower parents to participate
  meaningfully in the educational process.
- Convene a planning summit of local
  government, grassroots organizations, clergy, and
  public school officials to devise a plan to replace
  the current dysfunctional school board. Establish
  criteria for school board membership, including
  selection and removal.
- Create five- and ten-year capital plans to
  upgrade, renovate, and construct state-of-the-art
  school facilities. Devise a short-term plan to
  remove trailers.
- Partner with businesses, colleges and universities,
  and grassroots community-based organizations

to embrace and value education as a community obligation.

In 1955, the Montgomery Improvement Association played a pivotal role in a bus boycott that lasted for 381 days. How long are you prepared to plan and promulgate policies and programs to improve opportunities for a sound education for children living in Hempstead?

BRAINWASH BLACK BOYS TO BRILLIANCE

BY DR. BERNARD GASSAWAY, ORIGINALLY PUBLISHED IN HUFFPOST, AUGUST 13, 2016

I state the problem, offer seven strategies to address the problem, and conclude.

Problem

Choose any major urban city and the data on Black boys is the same: **Negative**. According to one Harvard University sociology professor, prison is predictable for Black boys: "About two-thirds of African-American men with **low levels of schooling** will go to prison in their lifetime." A 2015 PEW study revealed that even when the **poverty** rate slightly declined for most Americans, it remained relatively steady for Black children.

In addition to prison, poverty, and poor schooling, negative stereotypes, statistics, and perceptions abound in the media about Black boys. Images of Black boys as being delinquent and defiant, wayward and worthless, uncaring and unintelligent, cruel and criminal, vicious and violent, stubborn and stupid, immature and incapable, dark and deceptive, a gangbanger and a goon, a thug and a terrorist, and unskilled and unemployed are ingrained in the psyches of millions of Americans.

As these stereotypes are accepted, it becomes easier for people to literally and metaphorically destroy and kill Black boys with apathy or impunity. Some Black boys unwittingly embrace these negative portrayals and engage in reckless and dangerous behaviors.

I contend that "they" intentionally **indoctrinate** Black boys to accept the negative stereotypes that have retarded and continue to retard their development. Jawanza Kunjufu's classic work *Conspiracy to Destroy Black Boys* is as relevant today as it was when it was first published in 1985.

Strategies to Brainwash Black Boys to Brilliance

President Barack Obama's My Brothers Keeper Initiative was born out of the aforementioned reality faced by far too many Black boys. While the root causes of these alarming and **often repeated** statistics are the historic challenges of race, class, and economics, we can begin to implement strategies to redress many of the adverse effects of social policy and practices. I recommend the following seven strategies as a start.

- **Train** Black boys in the community to embrace their brilliance. Intentionally **indoctrinate** them to believe that they are:
  Brilliant, persistent, ambitious, sincere, motivated, bright, educated, courageous, tenacious, perspicacious, sagacious, adroit, thoughtful, gifted, conscientious, contemplative, spiritual, strong, diligent, tolerant, trustworthy, proper, determined, deliberate, insightful, intelligent, loving, caring, humble, prayerful, enthusiastic, respectful, innovative, reliable, imaginative, and resilient.

- **Learn** from the rhythms, beats and linguistics of hip hop music that have influenced youth cultures around the world to **persuade** and **convince** Black boys that they are brilliant.

- **Acquire** knowledge from the National Basketball Association about how it convinces millions of Black boys that a professional basketball career is highly likely, even when the odds are astronomically highly not likely. Utilize techniques that advertisers use to **sway** and **seduce** children to buy expensive sneakers, electronic games, and food products after watching or listening to a commercial on television or radio to **teach** Black boys to believe in their brilliance.

- **Design** curricula/lessons that can be taught in school, at home, and in the community to reinforce positive and enriching culturally relevant experiences that emphasize and instill pride in Black boys.
- **Teach** Black boys to affirm their brilliance. *"I affirm that I am brilliant! I value education (thinking and learning) as a means to make my family, my community, and me stronger. I strive for success to leave a lasting legacy for future generations to build upon. I strive never to harm others or myself. I strive to achieve my highest potential and promise."*
- **Develop** action plans (engage community leaders, educators, parents, clergy, mentors, and brothers-keepers) to **engage** Black boys in experiences that require them to broaden their mental, spiritual, and physical horizons.
- **Provide** Black boys with evidence of their brilliance by sharing information about their brilliant ancestors: Louis Armstrong, Ray Charles, Lewis H. Latimer, George Washington Carver, Imhotep, Charles R. Drew, Jesse Owens, Muhammad Ali, John Henrik Clarke, John Hope Franklin, Nelson Mandela, Haile Selassie, Toussaint Louverture, Hannibal Barca, Olaudah Equiano, Chinua Achebe, Benjamin Banneker, and Elbert Frank Cox.

Conclusion

Carter G. Woodson, father of Black History Month and author of *The Mis-Education of the Negro* said it best:

"If you can control a man's thinking you do not have to worry about his action. When you determine what a man shall think you do not have to concern yourself about what he will do. If you make a man feel that he is inferior, you do not have to compel him to accept an inferior status, for he will seek it himself. If you make a man think that he is justly an outcast, you do not have to order him to the back door. He will go without being told; and if there is no back door, his very nature will demand one."

It is necessary to take **control** of our Black boys' thinking. It is our moral responsibility to teach them **how to think**; in extreme times and circumstances, it is also necessary to teach them **what to think**.

Remember our Black boys learn by seeing and doing. They need to see you behave as you expect them to behave. They need to see that you practice what you preach. They need to be actively engaged by you daily to counteract the subliminal and overt negative stereotypes that influence how they are perceived and how they behave.

We need to do whatever is necessary to protect and nurture Black boys so they can grow to become healthy Black men.

Parents, You Have a Right to School Choice

by Dr. Bernard Gassaway, originally published in New York Amsterdam News, July 2, 2015

I attended primary and secondary public schools in New York City. I attended public, private and parochial colleges and universities in New York. I served as a public school teacher, assistant principal, principal and superintendent in New York City. I taught in public and private colleges in New York. While I wholeheartedly support public schools, I also support school choice. My wife and I chose not to send our only child Atiya to public school. We opted instead to homeschool her because we were not satisfied with the limited options that the public school system offered.

Seventeen years ago, my wife and I toiled over what we knew would be one of the most important decisions of our lives. How would we educate Atiya? We thought we would either enroll her in private or public school. We decided to enroll her in a school that was Montessori-like. We soon learned that none of the teachers were trained in the Montessori method. We withdrew Atiya and enrolled her in another private school.

When she was given a first-year teacher who did not know her name and could not tell us about her progress after six months, we chose to take her out of that private school. We then contemplated enrolling her in public school. Our public school option was limited to one neighborhood school, which seemed ideal. However, the school had a lottery and a waiting list. It was a very popular K-2 grade school, ideal for our small-framed, precious child. When we realized that this school was not an option for Atiya, we decided to homeschool her rather than enroll her in a public school that we believed would not meet her needs or our expectations.

As two working parents, we exercised choice without concern for tax credits, vouchers or charters. This, I am certain, is the case for many parents who choose not to send their children to traditional public schools. However, there are parents who do not have the financial ability to similarly exercise choice. Unfortunately, many poor and uninformed parents are led to believe that a traditional public school is the only option they have or need. They are made to feel bad if they consider enrolling their children in schools outside of traditional public schools, including public charter schools.

When I served as a principal and superintendent, I was often asked how I could homeschool my daughter when I was a principal in a public school. My answer was simple: I have a right to exercise choice. I was never told, nor did I ever believe, that I was obligated to enroll my daughter in public school as a condition of my employment. While some believed our decision was contradictory, we saw it as an exercise in freedom. As citizens, we had a right not to enroll our child in a school system we believed was not good for her. We knew of individual schools that were probably good for her; however, it was nearly impossible to enroll her without pulling strings, which I refused to do.

Today, when it comes to school choice, many public school parents are confused and even misinformed by school and elected officials. They are further confused by the vortex that is created when business, politics, religion and education mix. Consider the following: Which of these choices is the best education option for New York's children and families? (A) Charter, (B) Private, (C) Public, (D) Tax-Credit/Voucher or (E) All of the above?

All of the above could be correct. Why force parents to choose only one when a hybrid of approaches might produce the best of all possible worlds? If the current system does not work for the majority of children from low socio-economic backgrounds, which it does not, why continue to tinker with it under the guise of "reform" and "renewal"?

Here's what we know. Public schools will not improve significantly in New York unless change occurs in Albany.

The fate of more than 2 million children each year lies in the hands of legislators who fail to create laws and policies to help improve public schools, in part because of the stranglehold that unions have on them. As Gov. Andrew Cuomo and teachers' unions battle for control of the public school system, legislators nervously and strategically wait to see who will emerge as the winner. The safe bet is on the unions, because they will be around long after Cuomo leaves office.

With few exceptions, local politicians and public school officials remain relatively mute on public school choice. They dare not risk upsetting the status quo. They are afraid to take any position that would be opposed by the powerful teachers' unions. This is a sad but true reality.

Ironically, many public officials, including school personnel, who limit school choice options for poor and educationally disenfranchised parents exercise choice for their families. Do not be fooled by officials who support public school as the only option because their children are enrolled in public schools. While this may technically be true, many of their children are enrolled in public schools that operate as private schools. It is easier to enroll in some exclusive private schools than it is to enroll in some of the elite public schools that their children attend.

As a parent of a homeschooled child, I thank God that my wife and I were not persuaded by people who have been brainwashed to believe that public school should be the only option. I encourage all parents to exercise the right to vote and demand school choice for their children.

I also encourage members of the clergy to use their pulpits to inform parents about school choice.

Parents: Politicians and school officials depend on your lack of knowledge and complacency to continue their monopolistic public education system, which, by most accounts, fails hundreds of thousands of children annually. Do not be misled by Cuomo and Mayor Bill de Blasio's rhetoric and believe that tinkering with schools will bring about real progress. When you change the system, you change the schools.

The governor, mayor and public officials share the blame equally, as do you if you continue to remain silent and uninvolved. Fight for your right to exercise school choice, and then stay involved throughout your child's educational journey. Remember, people count on your absence to deprive and neglect your children with impunity!

Do Black Men Matter in Urban School Leadership?

by Bernard Gassaway, originally published in Gotham Gazette, October 29, 2014

AFTER a year of social unrest centered particularly around the killings of Black men and boys across this country, I find myself pondering what role, if any, Black male educational leaders play in preparing Black boys for what is happening to them and for what they are doing to each other? These questions came to light for me after the unrest in Baltimore, which appeared to hit a high when the youths of Baltimore expressed their dissatisfaction with the murder of Freddie Gray by setting the community ablaze.

First, I wondered: where were the Black male educational leaders in Baltimore when the unrest was occurring? What strategies, if any, did they implement to address the unrest with the children? If they took specific actions, might it be helpful for other communities to know what they did? We know from media accounts that grassroots individuals, parents, politicians, and clergy took to the streets to quiet the storm.

What happened when the children returned to school? Were teachers trained to lead discussions about the conditions that led to the unrest? Was there a curriculum provided to teachers to plan appropriate lessons? Did the teachers believe they were ready and able to discuss race vis-à-vis murder and unrest?

Looking at Ferguson, Chicago, Milwaukee, Brooklyn, Staten Island, Phoenix, North Charleston, and Cleveland made me think about Black male leadership in education in New York State (NYS) and New York City (NYC). I know from personal experience as a twenty-five-year urban school educator in NYC that educators are not prepared or trained to discuss race, riots, or unrest related to killings of Black men and boys.

Are Black male educational leaders in NYS and NYC, if they exist to any significant degree, responsible for initiating training for teachers' vis-à-vis writing curriculums and leading discussions that center on race and poverty? Would Black male educational leaders be prepared to engage with urban youths if the unrest experienced in Baltimore occurred in any major city in New York? Does it matter whether Black men are involved in the highest level of educational leadership in NYS and NYC?

Where is Black male leadership in NYS and NYC public education? Does any evidence exist that having

Black men at the table matters when public education
is discussed and when policies, standards, curriculums
and assessments are written, particularly related to racial
and social conditions that may lead to organized and
unorganized protests?

Does it matter whether Black men are involved at the
highest levels of public education in New York? Does it
matter to the governor of New York, the mayor of NYC,
or the chancellor of NYC's public schools? Does it matter
to you?

Do any Black men currently sit on NYS Governor
Andrew Cuomo's education leadership team? I believe
NYC Mayor Bill de Blasio has one on his school leadership
team. Does NYC Schools Chancellor Carmen Farina have
any? Does it matter?

What difference, if any, does it make having Black
men engaged at the highest levels of leadership in public
education? Should Black men have a role in writing
education policy and curriculums? Should Black men be
involved in the school-choice debate in New York? Should
Black men have a role in deciding how to spend billions
of dollars on education in New York? Should Black men
decide which community-based organizations are given
contracts to work with children and families, particularly
related to social conditions that lead to violence? Does it
matter?

Does the absence of Black men at the highest levels
of education leadership affect the quality of education

for Black boys, in particular? What message, if any, does the absence of Black men send to Black boys about their futures? This rang loudly for me as I watched the media accounts of the unrest in Baltimore.

As we undergo another round of education reform at the state and local levels in NYS and NYC education, perhaps the new state commissioner of education will determine whether Black men have a role at her table. Perhaps, the schools chancellor of NYC will be asked to address the presence of Black male leadership on her leadership team.

At a NYS learning summit convened by the NYS Regents (May 2015), six panels weighed in on teacher-evaluation policy. Not one Black man participated on any of the panels. Why not? Does it matter?

At the city level, the chancellor of NYC Schools apparently has decided that Black men do not have a seat at her central leadership table. Nor do they have a seat as a director at the newly formed Borough Field Support Centers. Of the seven centers, none of the directors are Black men. Why not? Does it matter?

Does it matter whether state and city urban school agendas include Black men to any significant degree? If they were present, what role, if any, would they play in educating the public, particularly our youths, about the role that race and poverty play in the killing of Black men and boys?

As the killings, whether through gun violence or through police action, continue throughout the United

States, I recommend that the governor of NYS, the mayor of NYC, and the chancellor of NYC public schools engage in public discussion and action to answer the question of whether having Black men involved at the highest levels of public education in New York matters? If it matters, they should take appropriate action to demonstrate its significance and not wait for the next killing.

I recommend that the clergy, the community, and elected officials engage in significant action to determine whether Black men matter in urban public school leadership. If it matters, they should advocate and act accordingly.

I pray that we not wait for the next series of killings to determine whether Black men in educational leadership have a specific and significant role to play in working to prevent the violence that is likely to surface as a direct result of our failure to educate our children and our community.

Based on the deafening silence about the absence of Black men in urban school leadership, one might easily conclude that having Black men in educational leadership does not matter.

Open letter to Mayor de Blasio: Plan to Succeed

by Bernard Gassaway, originally published in the New York Amsterdam News, November 13, 2014

NEW York City is not alone in facing a crisis in education. You have an opportunity to lead the nation in real education reform. It will require that you take extreme but prudent actions.

You must begin with a plan. You currently do not have a comprehensive plan to address the struggling school system. Your announced community school plan is one small step in the right direction. However, I believe you will have a major problem with scaling up the plan, largely because you do not have the leadership infrastructure within the Department of Education to implement it successfully on such a large scale.

Here's what I recommend. Convene an education commission to create a comprehensive plan to improve the struggling school system. It is not enough to focus on 94 struggling schools when the actual number exceeds 500 schools. These schools are predominately in poor and African-American communities.

Use your authority as mayor to bring all relevant city agencies into the education discussion. City agencies get failing grades for communicating and collaborating with the DOE. Fix the communication problem; collaboration will follow. The education solution will not come from Tweed—school officials currently function in too many silos. Increase your capacity by holding agency heads accountable for coming up with strategies to be included in your education plan.

Recruit conscientious African-American men to serve on the chancellor's leadership team. The fact that there are no African-American men on her cabinet is disturbing, given the fact that African-American boys are disproportionately left behind in the school system.

Develop a plan to train parents to become partners in education. This training is particularly necessary to support parents who are socioeconomically deprived. Enlist private, college/university and community partners to help with this work. Parents must play an integral role in any education plan.

Understand that students are struggling with Common Core because teachers are struggling. According to 2013–2014 citywide results for state reading and mathematics tests, only 28.4 percent of third through eighth graders are reading at or above grade level. This means that 71.6 percent are below grade level. Only 34.2 percent of students in those grades are at or above grade level for mathematics. The numbers for African-Americans (18.1 percent for reading, 18.6 percent for math) and special needs students (6.7 percent for reading and 11.4 percent for math) are even more staggering. These data are evidence that hundreds of schools are struggling, disproportionately affecting African-American males.

Examine how school leaders are trained to interpret student data. The current discussion is likely to drive some school faculty to cheat and to target the lowest performing students for removal to improve the data picture. What reportedly happened at Boys and Girls High School is a case in point. The current administration was accused of pushing out off-track students to improve the graduation rate for June 2015. This accepted DOE practice disproportionately affects African-American males.

Examine the work we began at BGHS during my tenure. You will find evidence of your espoused approach. In May of 2014, we partnered with Lutheran Family Health Center to open a comprehensive school-based medical clinic at BGHS. Over the past four years, we developed effective school-community partnerships with various partners to provide needed services to our students and families. We began a Young Adult Borough Center. We partnered with District 79 to bring career and technical education programs to BGHS. I know from experience that the community school approach works.

Examine how your community school plan is in conflict with the recent United Federation of Teachers collective bargaining agreement. Teacher contact time with students has been reduced because of the required 80- to 75-minute Monday and Tuesday professional development and parent outreach components. Renegotiate.

Examine the companies that are providing professional development to schools and principals: What evidence do they provide to prove that their approach works? From my experience, many of them do not have evidence. They get contracts because of their past affiliations with DOE officials.

Enlist college and university partners to work with schools to develop individualized "reform" plans. Schools that are saddled with incompetent staff are incapable of creating plans to improve themselves. The most effective strategy is to swiftly remove incompetent staff and replace them with competent staff. Your current plan recycles incompetent staff, which will perpetuate failure.

You have less than three years to fix a flawed, failed, struggling school system. Use your relationship with the education unions to convince or to pressure them to change their approach to protecting incompetence. To date, your team has been too slow, too shortsighted and too clandestine. You must act boldly, broadly and coura-geously with all deliberate speed before you run out of time.

OP-ED – OUR TIME PRESS

BY BERNARD GASSAWAY, ORIGINALLY PUBLISHED IN OUR TIME PRESS, OCTOBER 9, 2014

I began my career in the New York City Public School System in 1986 as an elementary school teacher. I became Senior Superintendent of Alternative Schools and Programs in 2003. I worked under the leadership of several mayors and chancellors. I left the system in the Bloomberg-Klein era in 2005 because I did not believe in their policies, particularly as they related to poor urban students. I returned to the system in 2009 to lead a transformation or turnaround of Boys and Girls High School.

Five years later, I reflect on the question of New York City Mayor de Blasio's plan for turning around struggling or failing schools. From my experience as the principal of Boys and Girls High School, a school identified being persistently low achieving, there is no plan. Unfortunately, when a plan is written, I have little hope for its success largely because the mayor and the current city school's chancellor Carmen Fariña are not seeking to address the underlining reasons for schools needing a turnaround plan. Furthermore, the chancellor does not appear ready to engage all stakeholders in the process of improving the entire school system. In my opinion, nothing will change in the absence of collaboration and coherent planning supported by timely and appropriate sustainable levels of funding.

As a current principal undergoing the so-called turnaround process, I have little hope for success, largely because there is no comprehensive plan. I have not experienced genuine collaboration. The current practice of DOE is to draft a plan, and to ask the school leadership team to pretend they are involved in the planning process. When I questioned the elements of their "plan" for Boys and Girls High School, I was told indirectly that I could either accept the plan or leave.

I have learned that for any turnaround plan to work there must be alignment between what is said publicly and what is practiced behind the scenes. There must be trust, respect, effective communications, and collaboration. If the individuals who create the strategy, and carry it out do not establish trust, the turnaround process is destined to fail. If individuals in the school and community feel dismissed and disrespected, they will not participate in the strategy and it will fail. If no one feels like they are being heard, the strategy will fail. If collaboration is top-down and the "real plan" is devised by central DOE personnel and imposed on the school, the strategy will fail.

Before any plan is written, we must ask ourselves

why high schools such as Townsend Harris, Bronx High School of Science, Stuyvesant, Brooklyn Tech, and Staten Island Tech may ever need a turnaround strategy. Traditions and standards exist at these institutions. Education officials make conscious decisions not to tinker with those traditions and standards. Their enrollment policies, for example, have been consistent since the schools' inceptions. None of these schools is required to enroll the lowest performing students. If one were to force the end of such traditions and standards, the mayor and chancellor would take a political beating similar to what they took when they attempted to tinker with the chapter school movement.

The current DOE may have a vision or pillars, but they do not have a plan. Within the DOE, staff members are talking about the current chancellor. I am not sure if they are talking with her. There is a belief among school personnel that this chancellor does not take pushback kindly. As a result, people refuse to speak in fear of risking their careers. So, as in the tale "The Emperor Has No Clothes," educators are afraid to tell the chancellor she has no plan or that her ideas and decisions in the absence of a comprehensive strategic plan are taking us back to before the Bloomberg-Klein era.

The De Blasio-Fariña administration is using some of the same tactics that were used by the Bloomberg-Klein administration. With one exception, Bloomberg and Klein hired top marketing firms to rebrand the DOE over and over.

Over the last six months, there have been increased efforts on the part of members of the DOE for me to remain silent regarding the current direction of the DOE. During the Bloomberg-Klein era, there was little doubt about the direction of the DOE. The goal of the DOE was to corporatize, privatize, and promote charter schools as the alternative to "public" education. While many stood on either side of the issue, it was clear that every person had to take a side. This is not the case with the current De Blasio-Fariña era. Nearly one year into the administration, there is still no clear direction from the DOE. What is clear from my perspective is that school leaders, primarily principals, are expected to remain silent and wait.

I have chosen not to remain silent and not to wait because the current direction is unclear, specifically regarding BGHS and similarly situated urban schools. As I attempted to work with DOE officials, it became clear that they were not clear about how to correct the wrongdoings of the previous administration. As a result, their misdirected/misguided efforts further exacerbate the problems.

I have come to the decision that I cannot effectively lead BGHS under the current conditions. However, I do remain greatly concerned about the welfare our children. I am concerned how the school staff, parents, students, and community stakeholders may continue to accept disrespect from school leaders who refuse to practice what they preach.

In closing, I would be remiss if I did not at least mention the elephant in the room. Racism is regrettably at the heart of much of our struggles in education. Unfortunately, too many of our leaders are afraid to address racism for fear of being ostracized. As a result, our children continue to languish in a system that is not designed for them to succeed in ways not measured by flawed standardized test results.

The chancellor is known to say that the answers are in the room. Her most difficult decision will be whether to listen to what people have to say. I doubt that she will.

The real question is: What are you prepared to do if she doesn't listen?

Restart May Be No Start at Boys and Girls High School

by Bernard Gassaway, originally published in Patch, May 31, 2011

AS the leader of Boys and Girls High School, I am committed to collaborative leadership and have not made any decisions in isolation that would have fundamentally changed the essence of the school.

Since I have multiple stakeholders, I choose to consult with them prior to making any substantive decisions. In recent months, New York City Department of Education officials have approached me on two occasions to make important decisions regarding the future of Boys and Girls High School, without allowing adequate time for consultation with stakeholders.

In both cases, I refused to accept their urgency as mine. On the one hand, they encourage school leaders to establish meaningful partnerships with community and faith-based organizations; while on the other, they expect us to ignore stakeholders when important decisions must be made. I know in my heart and soul that the recent decision of the DOE to move forward with the Restart model is not the best option for Boys and Girls High School.

Given the fact that it appears to be the only option that comes with significant resources makes some people say, "Take it! It may be the best that we can do at this time." I find myself rejecting this position. Although I understand their logic, they must understand that there are unrealistic expectations that come with this additional funding.

As people present the argument that money is a primary reason to agree with the Restart model, I offer the following. You give a hungry man one million dollars and tell him he cannot use the money to buy food. How does the money solve his most urgent problem, hunger? The same can be said of Boys and Girls High School. If we receive millions of dollars and cannot hire highly effective staff, how does the money address our most urgent problem, incompetence?

Money only matters when you have autonomy and a good plan. It does not matter when its use is restricted. Understand that the majority of the $3.5 to $6 million grant that may come with Restart would be restricted, primarily, to professional development. Also know that companies are adept at writing proposals to match the available funding. It should be clear to all that the greatest commodity in education is school failure and ultimately student failure.

This is unfortunate. Money alone is not the answer. I have espoused that of all the models being offered, Turnaround would give us the best chance to speed-up the reform of Boys and Girls High School. While I defend all efforts to keep Boys and Girls High School open forever, I do not defend the right of incompetent staff to remain with children indefinitely. The current system enables a disproportionate number of incompetent teachers and administrators to find homes in certain schools.

These schools are eventually labeled, S.U.R.R., Persistently Dangerous, and Persistently Low Achieving. To identify Boys and Girls High School as Persistently Low Achieving is like blaming the victim. The solution is not to close our school but to rather remove the "cancer of incompetence" before it ravages the body to a point where it can no longer function or live.

The Turnaround model would help accomplish this goal.

I appeal to the United Federation of Teachers and NYC Department of Education officials to remain at the bargaining table until all options are reasonably negotiated. In the end, any model that we adopt must allow school leadership to aggressively address staff incompetence.

Any change must be substantive and sustainable. We cannot merely tinker with dysfunction. We cannot put a dollar figure on what is priceless: The education and well-being of our children.

ABOUT THE AUTHOR

A**LRIGHT** – so today we've got the honor of introducing you to Bernard Gassaway. We think you'll enjoy our conversation; we've shared it below.

Bernard, thanks for joining us, excited to have you contributing your stories and insights. Let's kick things off with talking about how you serve the underserved, because in our view this is one of the most important things the small business community does for society – by serving those who the giant corporations ignore, small business helps create a more inclusive and just world for all of us.

I began my teaching career in 1986 at the beginning of the crack epidemic. I was driven to the teaching profession because of the stress that I caused my mother when I was a student in the New York City public school system. My mother passed away in April of 1986. I began teaching in September of 1986. I specifically wanted to teach boys thinking I would spare mothers the stress that I caused for my mother. I was the typical wayward child. Fortunately, my mother got to see me get my act together and eventually graduate from college. This was particularly significant because my trajectory was graduating to prison.

As always, we appreciate you sharing your insights and we've got a few more questions for you, but before we get to all of that can you take a minute to introduce yourself and give our readers some of your back background and context?

In my capacity as educator, I have been given many labels. The one that initially caused me to pause was "radical educator." I earned this title because I was not the typical go along to get along educator. I served as teacher, assistant principal, principal, and superintendent in the New York City Public School System. I was surprised in each role that the notion of putting children first was a façade. I guess to put it more strongly, it was a lie. Guardians of the system espoused putting children first while their actions demonstrated otherwise. As an educator, I found myself fighting the very people who were supposed to support me in my role as educational leader. The fights were focused on getting the resources and funding for my under-served children and families. While the "system" expected me to be a team player, I could not see myself a player on any team that did not respect children and families, particularly those most deserving.

Can you share a story from your journey that illustrates your resilience?

As a public-school student, I was labeled special needs. While the label may have been warranted, there was no formal system in place to justify the label. I believe my experience in public schools played a part in my juvenile delinquency. This led me to several encounters with law officials and eventually I became court involved. In fact, when I was 15-years old, I was sent to a juvenile detention center for 18 months, only having to serve 8 months because of good behavior. Post this experience, I changed my friends and my attitude and went on to graduate from college and eventually earn three master's degrees and a doctorate in educational leadership from Columbia University's Teachers College.

Any stories or insights that might help us understand how you've built such a strong reputation?

I can attribute my current reputation to my consistency. I am an unwavering child advocate. While I have my share of detractors, I believe people appreciate my ability and willingness to fight the good fight for children and families. I have no illusions about the power of the "system." However, this has not stopped me from confronting injustice, particularly when children were the targeted victims.

[Canva Interview 2023]

Epilogue:
The Edge Manifesto

Dr. Gassaway's closing principles for educators, parents, and advocates:

1. Protect children over policy.
2. Speak truth—even when you're alone.
3. Lead with vision, not fear.
4. Know your name. Speak their names.
5. Be prepared to lose comfort to gain purpose.

"If you're not leading from the edge, you're not leading at all."

Published Works Cited

GASSAWAY, Bernard. "Brainwash Black Boys to Brilliance." HuffPost, 13 Aug. 2016.

---. Black Leadership Equals Hope for Educational Transformation. Our Time Press, 27 May 2021.

---. "Do Black Men Matter in Urban School Leadership?" Gotham Gazette, 29 Oct. 2014.

---. "Hempstead Community: Black Public School Children Don't Matter." HuffPost, 13 July 2017.

---. "Open Letter to Mayor de Blasio: Plan to Succeed." New York Amsterdam News, 13 Nov. 2014.

---. Op-Ed. Our Time Press, n.d.

---. "Parents, You Have a Right to School Choice." New York Amsterdam News, 2 July 2015.

---. "Public School Officials Are Artificially Inflating Graduation Rates. I've Seen It Myself." Education Week, 29 Aug. 2017.

---. "Restart May Be No Start at Boys and Girls High School." Patch, 31 May 2011.

---. "Schools & Race Relations: A Toxic Topic." Gassaway Word Blog, 1 Nov. 2016.

---. "The Public School System Is Rigged Against Poor and Black Children." HuffPost, 6 May 2017.

www.ingramcontent.com/pod-product-compliance
Lightning Source LLC
LaVergne TN
LVHW051508080426
835509LV00017B/1970